WATCHLIST

ALEX VICKERY-HOWE

CURRENCY PRESS
The performing arts publisher

S
A
P
T

SOUTH
AUSTRALIAN
PLAYWRIGHTS
THEATRE

CURRENCT THEATRE SERIES

First published in 2020
by Currency Press Pty Ltd,
PO Box 2287, Strawberry Hills, NSW, 2012, Australia
enquiries@currency.com.au
www.currency.com.au

in association with South Australian Playwrights Theatre

Typeset by Dean Nottle for Currency Press.
Cover art: Nicholas Ely Design.

Currency Press acknowledges the Traditional Owners of the Country on which we live and work. We pay our respects to all Aboriginal and Torres Strait Islander Elders, past and present.

A catalogue record for this book is available from the National Library of Australia

Contents

Introduction

There's a (possibly apocryphal) study on apathy I once read about, offering participants free dental examinations. Subjects were split into three groups and told their teeth were: (a) fine; (b) needed more attention; or (c) catastrophic, and could only be saved by adopting the most rigorous routine. There was a catch of course; this was a study in psychology, not dentistry, and researchers were eager to learn how subjects would respond. Returning three months later, the first group had relaxed, the second showed minor improvement, and the third group abandoned the project altogether. In the face of almost certain failure, they gave up.

Having survived a tornado, attacks by flying monkeys, and even a wicked witch or two, there is no doubt that young Dorothy Gale is not the giving-up type. But arguably her bravest act is to pull back the wizard's curtain and discover the truth for herself—because we know that once she does, there's no going back: Schrödinger's wizard is dead, and his magic can no longer save her. Most of us lead our lives far downstage from the curtain and all the horror that hides behind it. We carry on in studied ignorance, pretending not to hear the rumbling from backstage. Ours are performances so convincing we almost fool ourselves—even as smoke fills the stage, even as the curtains catch fire. We close our eyes to the world because there are things we would rather not see ... because then we'd have to act on them.

As protagonists go, Basil Pepper doesn't strike us as the brave type. Yet having glimpsed behind the curtain, in Alex Vickery-Howe's acerbic new satire, Basil is faced with a dilemma we've all done our best to ignore. How does one live an ethical life in full knowledge of the state of the world? What is our moral obligation to others now and in the future? What is our obligation to those 8.7 million other species we share the planet with? Because, frankly, up until now we've done a pretty sorry job. Having confronted similar moral precipices, Delia leaps into desperate, militant action, while Roger gives up, withdrawing into bourgeois concern. At first glance, neither Delia's nor

Roger's response seems appropriate—one goes too far; the other not far enough—yet, given the stakes, are Delia's actions really so extreme?

This summer the world looked on as Australia burned: the blaze laying waste to some ten million hectares and more than a billion animals. Such numbers are abstract, difficult to grasp, but the daily sight of exhausted firefighters, scorched koalas and a frightened citizenry donning face masks under a leaden sky, proved more difficult to ignore. Though written months earlier, *Watchlist* has proven frighteningly prescient.

For if this is the new normal, Vickery-Howe dares to wonder, when our leaders sip mai tais on the beach while the nation burns, might behaviour such as Delia's represent the only truly rational response? Or perhaps not. Perhaps there is still a middle way between inaction and extremism—perhaps that word is activism.

Last year scientists in London endorsed mass civil disobedience to force governments to take rapid action on climate change. Movements like Extinction Rebellion have helped to catalyse marches around the world, bringing cities to a halt as citizens demand immediate action from those who claim to represent them. The wheel is turning. But will it be enough?

Watchlist asks tough questions without easy answers. The play's genius lies in its fusion of black comedy and political nous, skewering both sides of the ideological spectrum. Left and right both appear as the other side sees them. The right are all shadowy goons, throttling free speech in the service of Industry, while the left are 'the sort of people who buy a KeepCup for their Nissan Armada', deluding themselves they've done enough.

This last summer was Australia's glimpse behind the curtain. *Watchlist* is a play that challenges us to confront it and not look away. The only thing that matters is what we do next.

Caleb Lewis,
February, 2020

Postscript

In the time between writing and publication, the play has already been overtaken by recent events as a global pandemic wreaks havoc on our lives, shutting down the systems we had so unthinkingly come to rely on—systems that ironically made such disaster possible. What seemed speculative only months back now feels disconcertingly prophetic. From incendiary summer to austere winter, the signs are clear: our way of life must fundamentally change. Existing paradigms are broken. Commenting on the spate of lockdowns crippling the globe, my sister wondered aloud today if Mother Nature might not have sent us to our rooms to think about our behaviour? And when the time comes to step outside again and breathe in, without fear of contagion, then we have an opportunity to change our ways before it's too late. Vickery-Howe's *Watchlist* is an urgent clarion call for action. We ignore it at our risk.

C.L.

Watchlist was first produced by South Australian Playwrights Theatre and programmed for a 2020 production. Due to the outbreak of COVID-19, the premiere took place as a radio play ahead of a 2021 live performance with the following cast:

BASIL	Gianluca Noble
MARIE	Katie O'Reilly
DELIA	Katherine Sortini
ROGER	Eddie Morrison
NORMAN	Matt Hawkins

Director, Lisa Harper Campbell
Producer, Lucy Combe
Lighting Designer, Stephen Dean
Sound Designer, Sascha Budimski
Stage Manager, Clare Miyuki Guerin
Set Construction, David Adams

CHARACTERS

BASIL PEPPER, early 20s, male, browbeaten, gangly, and often perplexed. Baz is trying to better himself in a discordant world.

MARIE HARBUCK, 40s-50s, female. Basil's mum, small in stature, but supremely confident and casually withering.

DELIA DENGEL, mid 20s, female. A forthright and passionate environmental activist ... kind, but clawed.

ROGER THE KNOB, hitting 30, male. Basil's housemate, disdain in a lilac dressing-gown.

NORMAN GOULD, 40s-50s, male. ASIO's fifth-best man; they don't let him carry a weapon.

SNOOPS, intelligence operatives.

SETTING

We're not hiding anything. This is an unashamedly theatrical space, where the stage crew are often in full view of the audience, even interacting with the characters. Each is an extension of Norman Gould: sinister flunkies in tailored suits, skivvies and regulation shades. We call them Snoops.

There is little to no break between scenes, the action driven musically and performatively. If props are still coming in, we barrel on. Occasionally, setting and mood changes are punctuated by choreographed routines, emphasising the artifice of the stage. Most of these sequences are tight and comedic ... although some, with seductive or ominous undertones, may linger.

Tonally, we're skating between romantic farce and film noir. Scenes tend to alternate in this way, but there is darkness throughout. Shadows are the primary set dressing.

Among the silliest moments, there's still something wistful—something melancholy—pushing in at the edges.

Something is being lost.

This play went to press before the end of rehearsals and may differ from the play as performed.

'We are, quite literally, gambling with the future of our planet—for the sake of hamburgers.'

Peter Singer

ACT ONE

GETTING OUT

BEFORE THE SHOW ...

'Manchild' by Neneh Cherry plays.

A figure paces in the gloom, becoming increasingly agitated ... turning, kicking, turning, smacking his head, turning ...

This is it.

This is the end of the line.

The last stop.

And there's something weird about this guy. Something about his outfit. Is that ... a plush lizard costume?

A chameleon?

He paces like Barney the dinosaur, if Barney ever had anger management issues.

He mopes.

He rages.

He sinks.

Broken. Spent. Trapped.

It all ends not with a bang, but with a blubber.

He curls up within a clutching canopy of prison bars—silhouetted—like fingers tightening, squeezing the sunlight away.

SCENE ONE

A room of shadows.

BASIL *calls, plaintively, in the dark.*

BASIL: Hello? Is anybody ... Look, guys, I need to tinkle.

    Silence.

I haven't been charged with anything! You can't just ... well, I don't *think* you can ... there are rules, aren't there?!

Still nothing.

Alright, I'm unzipping. *I'm unzipping!* S'all gonna happen now! It won't be nice!

He unzips.

I mean it!

Beat.

Timid bladder.

He zips himself up.

I want a phone call. You can't deny me that! [*To the sky*] Fascists!

A door opens.

One hell of a creak. BASIL *shrinks away ...*

Slivers of light expose a small desk, two chairs and a dated tape recorder.

Don't hit me, man! You can't! *It's against the rules!*

NORMAN GOULD *enters. He's just another shadow in the room ... slender, willowy ... but when he reaches out to switch on a hanging light bulb, his true visage swims into being.*

NORMAN: Rules, Mr Pepper? My, how we've grown.

BASIL: [*relieved*] Norm, thank heavens.

NORMAN: You didn't care about the rules when you were free-range. Now that I have you ensnared, you imagine we'll all return to civility ... [*A grim smile*] That's not the way it works, Mr Pepper. Not the way *I* work.

His hand snaps up and steadies the bulb.

NORMAN *is one of a kind. David Lynch hair. Black skivvy. Bespoke suit. He thinks he's Agent Smith.*

He isn't.

BASIL: Tell them this is a misunderstanding. You know I'm not a criminal, Norm!

But NORMAN *has his eyes fixed on the bulb.*

NORMAN: Civilisation requires accountability.

> *The bulb hangs still.*

Accountability requires justice.

> *He turns and leans over the desk, pinning* BASIL *with rapier eyes.*

Justice requires me.

> *Their faces are close. Weirdly so.*

> BASIL *breaks away first.*

BASIL: I'm not scared.

NORMAN: No?

> *Straight-faced—a sense of humour is anathema to this guy—* NORMAN *becomes a slender shadow once more, sliding over to the far corner of the room.*

> *Pipes gurgle as he twists on a tap and lets the water run.* BASIL *holds his bladder, wincing …*

How do you feel now, Mr Pepper?

BASIL: Low blow.

NORMAN: Perhaps if I increase the temptation …

> *He twists the tap harder.*

BASIL: *Shut it off! Please!*

NORMAN: I'm not a violent man, Mr Pepper … but I have catalogued your every weakness.

BASIL: *This isn't fair!*

> NORMAN *turns off the tap.*

NORMAN: You wet yourself in Miss Heartwig's tepid production of *Les Misérables.*

BASIL: [*outraged*] I did not.

> *Beat.*

I pissed in the trombone.

NORMAN: And, again, in Professor Taffy's physics lecture … when you were old enough to have more control.

> *As he rumbles the word 'control',* NORMAN *curls his leather glove into a fist, staring down at* BASIL *with Darth Vader intensity.*

He refuses to blink.

I know *everything*.

BASIL: This is cruel and unusual punishment. I have—

NORMAN: You *don't* have rights, Mr Pepper. Officially, you're not even here. You're at home painting orcs and goblins.

> BASIL *swallows.*

BASIL: That's unnervingly specific.

NORMAN: You're petting your goldfish, Señor Flapsy.

BASIL: How do you pet a—?

NORMAN: [*stalking him*] You're pacing the cupboard you call a condo and praying that fortunes will turn, you're reading Fred Basset comics and asking your friends to decipher them, you're whining, you're trolling, you're wasting the divine gift of sentient life in a sad quarter acre of crapulence and depravity far, far away from people who count for something, who *contribute*.

> *The words are savage, swift, but perfectly enunciated.* NORMAN *unbuttons his cuffs and rolls up his sleeves.*

> *Fire becomes ice.*

You're being *you*, Mr Pepper. Shiftless. Disorderly. *Absurd.*

> *He sits opposite* BASIL *and—sorta, more or less—smiles.*

But you're not here.

> *He knits his gloved fingers.*

So, how can you be in distress?

> *Long beat.*

> *Enmity crackles between the two men.*

> BASIL *lets out a sigh. He pulls his lizard hood back, revealing a youthful yet careworn face.*

BASIL: Can I at least have my gum?

NORMAN: …

BASIL: [*prompting*] My gum. Juicy Fruit. There were two tabs left in my coat po—

> NORMAN *drops the gum in his mouth and chews. It's borderline orgasmic.*

Oh, that's thoughtful. That's a simple pleasure. Gone.

> NORMAN *winces.*

Sour cherry. Limited edition. I know it stings. [*Leaning back, smug*] Some people don't have the balls for it.

> BASIL *winks, savouring the upper hand.*

> NORMAN *picks up a wastepaper basket and spits out the gum.*

What can I tell you? It's an acquired—

NORMAN: You're in trouble, Mr Pepper. You're sinking into a deep molasses.

BASIL: Shut up, Norm. You're hardly a butch guy.

NORMAN: [*nettled*] Did you not notice the gloves?

BASIL: My mum is like sixteen times scarier than you.

> *Beat.*

NORMAN: She is.

BASIL: Just be straight, alright? What do you think I've / done?

NORMAN: Don't act dopey, Mr Pepper.

BASIL: It's *not* an act. People say it is, but—

NORMAN: Where did she find you?

BASIL: Where did who—?

NORMAN: The recruiter! The seditionist! [*Lasciviously*] Your little gateway drug.

> *The penny hits the floor.*

BASIL: Is this about my girlfriend? She has a name.

NORMAN: She has a record.

BASIL: She's five foot nothing … and chirpy.

NORMAN: You have *both* been identified as a grave threat.

BASIL: *To what?!*

> BASIL *is on his feet.*

> NORMAN, *still seated, noticeably shrivels.*

I'm not impressed by you. Touch one hair on her brilliant head and you'll see just how 'disorderly' your life can become.

> *This time it is* BASIL *who refuses to blink.* NORMAN *placates him, arms spread.*

NORMAN: This is, as you say, a civilised country. We *do* have rules and we don't detain citizens merely for being cretinous louts. [*Clearing his throat*] Has it not occurred to you that Delia may, in fact, be dangerous?

BASIL: No.

NORMAN: There was nothing convenient about your shared diversions? New Order? Alphaville?

BASIL: That's just good taste in—

NORMAN: Vintage helicopters? Delft pottery?

> BASIL *takes the blow. It does sound fishy when he thinks about it. He turns away.*

BASIL: Again, unnervingly specific.

NORMAN: Oh, she was. Even more than I.

BASIL: [*with a shrug*] It's chemistry.

NORMAN: Is it?

BASIL: …

NORMAN: You're not so certain anymore, are you?

> *The power balance tips.* BASIL *resumes his seat.* NORMAN *rises and circles the desk …*

You know how you found your way onto *my* list, Mr Pepper … but have you not paused to wonder how Delia selected you? And for what purpose?

> *His finger touches the recorder. Spools turn.*

I shall ask you one more time. Where—?

BASIL: Dad's funeral. She found me at Dad's funeral.

> BASIL *sinks deep into his chair. He looks up at* NORMAN, *haunted.*

> NORMAN *clasps his hands behind his back, relishing his first baby step towards victory.*

> *And everything changes … 'Daddy Cool' by Boney M. kicks in.*

> *The room of shadows becomes a neon Rubik's cube, burning with colour. We're going back in time.*

SCENE TWO

The music is very loud and there are lots and lots, and lots, of lights. Gloomy tiles are replaced by a flashing disco floor. The desk, the chairs and the recorder are snatched away, but we don't care because ...

Downstage left, ROGER THE KNOB *has appeared, buttoning his tux. And what a tux. White, with a purple corsage—a chrysanthemum. He complements his threads with the smuggest smile conceivable, stretching from cheek to cheek. In one hand he holds a hefty Bible, in the other a can of hairspray. He preens himself.*

Downstage right, MARIE HARBUCK *fixes her veil. She is in mourning, dabbing her eyes with a tissue before letting the veil fall across her chalky features.*

ROGER *adds volume to his hair. Checks his Bible verse. All set.*

MARIE *reaches for her coat and drapes it, stylishly, across her shoulders. No, that's not working ...*

ROGER *spies a zit. Curses. Pops it.*

MARIE *replaces her coat with a cape, swishing it grandly ... and not quite as mournfully as she should.*

ROGER *sniffs his underarms. Fuuuck!*

MARIE *turns, lifts her veil and checks her buns out in her skirt.*

ROGER *sprays cologne.*

MARIE *wiggles.*

Both spin, synchronously, and head upstage where ... a coffin has appeared.

BASIL *has appeared too. He has squeezed himself into a black suit—not nearly as flamboyant as* ROGER*'s tux, but far more appropriate.*

Unlike the others, BASIL *is genuinely heartbroken. He lovingly dusts the coffin and lays out snacks.* SNOOPS *may assist, feigning sadness; their gloomy expressions completely at odds with the music.*

MARIE *crosses over to* BASIL *and meets him centre stage. Neither knows what to do next. If they hug, it is weird and stilted ... they may settle for shaking hands.*

Beside them, ROGER *scoops up some Tim Tams and wipes his fingers on the mortcloth.*

BASIL *notices and shoots a glare* ROGER*'s way.*

ROGER *nods solemnly and makes a beeline for the pulpit. Once he has the whole room's attention, however, he can't resist a boogie.*

We realise 'Daddy Cool' isn't artistic license ... this is actually what's playing at the funeral.

BASIL*, oblivious, finds a quiet pew and smothers his face.*

Among the mourners, we may spot DELIA DENGEL—*jet-black hair tied in two long plaits down to her navel, love beads sparkling around her neck and both wrists. She alone looks at* BASIL *with compassionate eyes. He has yet to notice her ...*

But that will happen.

MARIE*, already bored, makes a slicing gesture across her own neck. The music cuts out.*

Painful silence.

ROGER *opens his Bible.*

ROGER: 'And He smote the men of Beth-shemesh, because they had looked into the Ark of the Lord.'

> *He glares down at the mourners.*

'He smote of the people fifty thousand and threescore and ten men … and the people lamented, because the Lord had smitten many of the people with a Great Slaughter!'

> *The Bible closes with an intimidating thud.*

Yeah, that's right. God killed fifty thousand men for looking at something.

> BASIL *peeks out from between his fingers. This has already shot off the rails.*
>
> ROGER *indulges him with a nod: 'Don't worry, I've got this, Baz'.*
>
> BASIL *shakes his head: 'No, no, you really don't.'*
>
> ROGER *takes in the room.*

Now, I don't know about any of you, but I'd think twice before defying that almighty hard-arse. God is great and God is nuts.

[*Crossing himself*] So, it is with humility, and maximum respect, that we make ourselves comfy in His great house this afternoon.

He gestures to the coffin.

Howard is comfy too. At long last.

BASIL *coughs deliberately.*

I first met Howard through his only son, Basil. Much like Jesus, my mate Baz was a precocious child who grew up with a taste for fine wine and adventure.

Another cough. BASIL *is trying to put an end to this.*

We shared a school bus for many happy years, Baz and I. Me at the back with the senior girls. Baz at the front with his imaginary friends … and Howard … well, Howard was always there. Waiting. At the bus stop.

DELIA *hands* BASIL *a glass of water.*

BASIL *accepts the glass, but keeps labouring the cough.* MARIE *nudges him.*

I know, mate. I get choked up too. [*Back to his notes*] What words can I use to describe Howard Pepper? [*With a shrug*] Fairly short. Inoffensive. I remember one time he borrowed my—

MARIE*'s phone rings. She doesn't notice.*

BASIL: Mum …

Heads turn.

Mum!

Beat.

MARIE: Oh, shit me.

She tunnels into her handbag.

BASIL: It's the centre button, the centre … give it.

MARIE *thrusts her handbag into* BASIL.

MARIE: Help your mother for once.

BASIL *peers into the bag. Nothing.*

He stares at MARIE.

…?

The phone warbles on.

BASIL: Pocket.

MARIE: Which?

BASIL: *Pocket!*

He fumbles into her dress pocket and withdraws the phone.

How do I unlock the / cover?

MARIE: I know this phone better than you.

She snatches it back.

BASIL *forces a pained, rictus smile.*

BASIL: You don't. You really don—

MARIE: Shush, this is a funeral service.

BASIL: I know that, Mum.

MARIE: You're quite selfish, Basil.

DELIA *reaches over, takes the phone and discreetly unlocks the cover. Beat.*

She nervously hands it back to MARIE, *who switches the phone off.*

[*To* BASIL] Why do I think you can do anything?

At the pulpit, ROGER *has frozen mid-story. He collects himself.*

ROGER: My lawnmower. Howard borrowed my … He liked to mow.

Flustered now, ROGER *returns to his Bible.*

'And the king said unto her, What aileth thee? And she answered, This woman said unto me, Give thy son, that we may eat him to day, and we will eat my son to morrow. So we boiled my son, and did eat him: and I said unto her on the next day, Give thy son, that we may eat him: and she hath hid her son …'

Beat.

While he was a devout Christian, Howard was not a cannibal. In this way, he diverted from the teaching …

MARIE *rattles a packet of Jaffas.* BASIL *shakes his head emphatically.*

BASIL: [*hissing*] Mum, no.

ROGER: ... but this was a testament to Howard's maverick edge. Never one to conform, Howard cut his own path. Indeed, his love of gardening ...

> MARIE *rips the packet open, sending Jaffas everywhere.*

... whether it be the roses in his front yard, or the succulents out back ...

BASIL: Leave them, Mum.

ROGER: ... was one of Howard's defining interests.

MARIE: No, these are Jaffas. These are good.

BASIL: *Mum!*

ROGER: He appreciated the fertiliser that I put together for him ...

> BASIL *wrestles with* MARIE *as she bends down to retrieve her Jaffas.*

MARIE: Three second rule.

ROGER: ... and for which I offered a competitive price.

BASIL: [*to* MARIE] No. [*To* ROGER] And no.

ROGER: Howard once told me ...

BASIL: I can see what you're doing, Roger.

ROGER: ... how much he enjoyed good value, and customer satisfaction ...

BASIL: *Roger.*

> *Beat.*

ROGER: Mondays through Thursdays. Website on the back of your program.

> *He returns to his Bible.*

God was also into human trafficking.

> BASIL *raises his voice.*

BASIL: Alright, that's enough. Can we ... can we have a hymn please? A pleasant hymn?

> MARIE *stands.*

MARIE: My husband will be interred with his mother. [*To* BASIL] Assuming she's actually there.

BASIL: She's there, Mum. [*To the room, smiling*] Grandma is there.

MARIE: Well, they *say* she's there, darling ... but when you're a bucket of ash people can take advantage.

BASIL: [*calling, desperately*] A hymn? One of the old classics?

> *Organ music plays.*

Cheers. That's nice.

> SNOOPS *gather around the coffin, paying their last respects.*

> BASIL *looks down at his toes. He's really feeling this moment.* MARIE *rubs his back.*

MARIE: How are your finances?

BASIL: …

MARIE: [*her eyes narrowing*] How are your finances?

BASIL: …

MARIE: You won't tell me?

BASIL: …

MARIE: Come on, spit it out. Just … is it bad?

BASIL: …

MARIE: How bad is it?

BASIL: …

MARIE: Basil—

BASIL: He's gone, Mum.

> *She nods.*

> *He wipes his eyes.*

> *Beat.*

> *She rattles the packet of Jaffas at him. He takes one.*

> *Lights fade.*

> *A single light bulb descends.*

SCENE THREE

NORMAN *stands under the bare bulb.*

NORMAN: And *she* was already there?

> *As before,* NORMAN *reaches up to steady the bulb.* BASIL *turns to face him. He nods.*

> *Everyone else has frozen …* ROGER *at the pulpit,* MARIE *with a Jaffa halfway between her lips …*

And DELIA, *standing off to the side, seemingly unimportant.*

You're certain of that much?

BASIL: I'd noticed her.

NORMAN: What had you noticed?

BASIL: She smelt like …

NORMAN: [*prompting*] You noticed her smell?

BASIL: Like the outdoors.

> BASIL *looks away.*

Like childhood.

NORMAN: Ah, she made you wander back to better days. She reminded you …

> *He approaches* DELIA.

… of your father, perhaps? [*Contemptuously*] With his green thumbs.

BASIL: I was suffocating.

NORMAN: Were you?

BASIL: The walls were closing in.

NORMAN: They'll close in again if you refuse to cooperate, Mr Pepper.

BASIL: I felt trapped. Delia was my way out.

NORMAN: Quite the opposite … But, by all means, share your love story.

> BASIL *runs his fingers through his hair, gathering his memories.*

BASIL: Later.

> *He exhales.*

The wake.

> NORMAN *steps back, into shadow. The light bulb recoils.*

SCENE FOUR

'Your Love Takes Me Higher' by The Beloved plays. The mood has shifted. Red lights. Electronica. Hormones.

Everyone is on their eighth drink.

ROGER *has become a DJ. Sweat shines from his forehead as he works his magic. His Bible has been exchanged for a microphone … and some kind of canary-coloured cocktail, bubbling toxically, packed with paper umbrellas.*

ROGER: [*over the microphone*] This one goes out to Howie P. Mention his name and we'll slash our prices!

Cheers all round.

ROGER *gives* BASIL *a smooth thumbs-up.*

The song brings SNOOPS *to the dance floor, where* MARIE *reigns. Her cape is somewhere around her ankles.*

BASIL *wanders, removed from it all, still punch-drunk by grief. But* SHE *is there.*

DELIA *moves, downstage left, her rhythm natural and confident. She dances like a sober person who actually likes dancing.*

BASIL *is drawn away from his pain, long enough to be mesmerised. He opens his mouth.*

He takes a step.

He thinks better of it.

He backs away.

He turns.

And ROGER *is there, gyrating like a psychopath.*

Dance with me, Basil!

BASIL *declines.*

ROGER *whips around him, waggling his finger.* DELIA *catches* BASIL*'s eye.*

She smiles.

BASIL *rolls his eyes at* ROGER*'s antics, but he's smiling now too.*

And maybe it's the alcohol, maybe it's the loss that lingers in the air, maybe it's just one of those magic nights ...

Whatever it is, BASIL *gives in to it.*

He and ROGER *fall into a routine. The Running Man. The Electric Slide. None of it is necessarily good—it's high school dancing, revisited.*

Still, there's joy in it.

DELIA *moves over to them, brushing by* ROGER *... fixing her gaze on* BASIL *...*

They move together. Comfortably goofy.

ROGER *returns to the microphone.*

[*Into the mic*] What am I drinking? *I don't know!*

More cheers.

DELIA *leans close to* BASIL *... and whispers in his ear.*

BASIL *watches, openly besotted, as she slinks to the exit.*

MARIE *taps him on the elbow.*

He turns back.

Just in time to catch his mother.

SCENE FIVE

Lights up. Stark. A white wash. BASIL *nurses* MARIE.

BASIL: You're alright.
MARIE: I'm a widower.
BASIL: [*with a sigh*] That too.

> *He guides her down to a pew, his eyes drifting back to the coffin.*
>
> *The music has left another heavy silence, this one broken by the occasional hiccup.*

MARIE: Great funeral.
BASIL: ...
MARIE: Headstone was exorbitant.
BASIL: That's not a thing you say, Mum.
MARIE: [*dismissing him*] I could hardly send your father off with a fistful of pebbles and some gaffer tape.

> BASIL *looks away.*

You know I loved him.

> *Beat.*

BASIL: I'll call an Uber.
MARIE: Basil, wait.
BASIL: ...
MARIE: We need to talk.
BASIL: [*gently*] I don't.

MARIE: About what happens.

BASIL: Happens?

MARIE: Now.

> *She sits up, reclaiming some dignity … if not sobriety.*

You could have chipped in, you know.

BASIL: [*thrown*] Are you seriously—?

MARIE: Don't you think it's time you stood up?

BASIL: *I'm* not the wobbly one.

MARIE: It's a metaphor, Basil. [*Abruptly curt, austere*] You need to get out of that head of yours.

BASIL: Today? We're doing this *today*?

MARIE: What kind of mother would I be if I allowed you to paint … now, I want to say 'oinks' …

BASIL: Orcs. They're called orcs, Mum.

MARIE: [*nodding*] Yes, very sad.

BASIL: It's a hobby.

MARIE: You don't get paid for it, do you, Basil?

BASIL: Oh, I see … I'm a burden, am I?

MARIE: You're not *anything*. Not employed. Not engaged.

BASIL: I'm an individual.

MARIE: Not aspiring. Not ambitious.

BASIL: I'm a gamer.

MARIE: Not involved.

BASIL: I'm a lizard enthusiast.

> *Beat.*

MARIE: You finished high school and just … stopped. I blame the career counsellor. She said you were unworkable.

BASIL: I have skills. They're waiting to be discovered.

> *He waggles his finger at her. Loses his confidence … bows his head.*

MARIE: Don't get upset.

BASIL: Why would I be upset, Mum?

MARIE: You need to pick a direction and march towards it.

BASIL: When have you *ever* supported me?

MARIE: Oh, whinge.

BASIL: You didn't believe in my pottery … my music …

MARIE: Darling, you peed in the—

BASIL: Again, with the trombone! I said I was sorry a zillion times!

MARIE *stands. Not all that well.*

MARIE: Do you have to make a scene in front of your father?

BASIL: He would take my side, he always did.

MARIE: Yes. [*To the coffin*] Ponce.

BASIL: Is this what we've come down to?

Both are addressing a dead man now.

MARIE: You wanted a baby. I wanted a beagle.

BASIL: She'd replace me with an oil painting just to save on soap and toothpaste!

MARIE: Why weren't you stricter with him?

BASIL: *What did you see in her?*

They exhale.

MARIE: [*sincerely*] I need to push him out of our nest.

Long pause.

BASIL, *heartbroken, turns and picks up his mother's cape. He plays with the stitching, avoiding her eye …*

Shame hardens into anger.

MARIE *turns her back on the coffin, reasoning with her son.*

I'm not being / cruel.

BASIL: You've been humiliating me my entire life!

She fobs him off.

MARIE: I don't think that's fair.

BASIL: What's my name, Mum?

Busted.

MARIE: I'm not engaging.

BASIL: Basil Pepper! Basil *fucking* Pepper!

Beat.

MARIE *can't help herself. She bloody loves this joke …*

Glee explodes from her diaphragm.

MARIE: I'm such a cock.

She laughs until her cheeks turn burgundy, and her ribs ache.

BASIL: Your first interaction with your only son … literally, the very, very first thing … was an act of ridicule, scorn and mockery.

MARIE: Noooo, that's not what … [*Laughing harder*] Yep. That's totally right!

BASIL stares in disgust, but MARIE isn't slowing down anytime soon. She pops both of her middle fingers and waves them around. It's part-dance, part-stumble.

He didn't even notice. Took him seven months. [*Cackling*] Dozy tit!

She hoots at the coffin.

BASIL breaks into a smile. He shakes his head.

This is his mum.

BASIL: You are a repulsive example of humanity.

MARIE: [*grinning*] Oh, Basil … Basil, Basil … Basil …

She wipes her eyes.

Please get out of my house.

BASIL nods, still smiling. He opens his arms to her … MARIE falls into them.

It's a new chapter. Has to be.

They sway together.

BASIL: This is like when an Egyptian pharaoh dies. They bury the cat too.

MARIE: You're better than a cat, Basil.

Beat.

BASIL: Thanks, Mum.

He opens his arms again, and sets her free.

Can we have a moment?

She nods, then …

MARIE: [*to the coffin*] Don't you dare contradict me.

Her wink is partly for BASIL; mostly for the man she's lost.

She collects her cape and swishes it around her shoulders once more.

How do I look?

BASIL: Like a supervillain.

> *Beat.*

[*Softening*] Like a queen.

> *He wants to say more, but doesn't know how. She rescues him.*

MARIE: You know I love you too, Basil.

> *He has never been more thankful. Nods. Blushes, even.*
>
> *She heads out.*
>
> *Turns back.*

I just don't want to live with you.

> *Lights change.*

SCENE SIX

Alone, more or less, BASIL *approaches the coffin.*

BASIL: Alright, Dad? Cosy?

> *No longer stark, the lights are dimming around him.*

You've left me with a lot to live up to.

> *His lip trembles.*

Too much.

> *It's sunset.*
>
> *The first, faint chords of 'Leave' by R.E.M. creep into being.*
>
> *So too does* NORMAN GOULD—*more wraith than man—his gloved fingers flexing, eyes sharp and suspicious as they find a thin ribbon of starshine.*

NORMAN: And so, you said your farewells … How stirring.

BASIL: Yes, and no. I told him I was proud. I told him I was grateful. [*Ashamed*] And I lied. I said I was ready to move on.

NORMAN: My sympathies, Mr Pepper, but none of this—

BASIL: [*ignoring him*] I'll do my very best, Dad. Hopefully it's enough.

DELIA: He's not there.

> NORMAN, *taken off guard, falls into a defensive stance.* BASIL *grins.*

BASIL: I told you. Delia was my way out.

> DELIA *stands in the doorway. Radiant and mischievous.* NORMAN *steps back, unsettled.*

NORMAN: What did you do next?

> DELIA *holds her hand out to* BASIL.

BASIL: The same thing you do, Norm …

> BASIL *walks towards* DELIA.
>
> *She beckons to him.*

   … I gave chase.

> *And they're off.*

SCENE SEVEN

The music kicks, epic as hell.

DELIA *and* BASIL *shoot across the stage, running from one side to the other, sprinting up the aisles, circling the auditorium, and all the way back again. Or perhaps they're running on the spot—breaking into the open air—as shadows fall away.*

They're making some distance, leaving the church behind …

Soon, the last rays sunset has to offer shift from orange to magenta, to a stormy blue.

Ripples of water shimmer over them both, punctuated by the smack of heavy rain. DELIA *laughs.*

BASIL, *unnerved but enchanted, offers her a smile.*

DELIA: [*over the rain*] He's out here! In the world!
BASIL: [*hollering back*] Who are you?!

> DELIA *turns and breaks into another sprint.* BASIL *rushes after her.*
>
> *He catches his breath.*
>
> *She lets him catch her too …*
>
> *They tumble and rise together, sliding back against the arch.*
>
> BASIL *releases her.*

She snatches his hand and brings it back to her waist. He has more questions.

Until she kisses him.

Cymbals clash as thunder rolls.

But just as soon as she appeared ... DELIA *vanishes, into the rain.*

SCENE EIGHT

MARIE: She left like Cinderella.

Lights up.

That hanging bulb.

NORMAN: Your boy doesn't see it ... but, evidently, she picked him. *Groomed* him.

MARIE: My 'boy' makes his own decisions. I didn't raise him to follow anyone blindly ... [*Enjoying herself*] I must be very different to your mother.

NORMAN has placed his jacket on the back of his chair. He looks tired, worn down by a sharper mind.

Opposite him, MARIE *has swapped her black funeral attire for a pantsuit and a vivid shawl. Her left arm hangs in a cast and sling. She winces, occasionally, but she won't be the one to sweat during this exchange.*

NORMAN: You work alone?

MARIE: There's a limit to how many humans I can cooperate with at any one time. Once it gets to double figures, I'm out.

NORMAN: Romantic fiction, that's your trade?

MARIE: You grew up on spy thrillers, didn't you? Connery? Moore? Who gets your end / wet?

NORMAN: Fascinating, is it not, that your son should live out one of your tawdry potboilers?

MARIE: Snob.

NORMAN: You can't shake me. I read people the way people read books.

MARIE: Fairytales don't count, Norm.

NORMAN: You'd like to believe that's what this is.

Slowly, NORMAN *reaches into his coat and withdraws a manila folder.*

Regrettably, Ms Harbuck, the stakes are very high … and, for once, your words will not be ignored.

> *Beat.*

MARIE: I bet it was Dalton. You crave the darker souls.
NORMAN: Occupational hazard.

> *He slides the folder across the desk.*

What drew Delia to your family?
MARIE: I don't know.
NORMAN: Why did she gravitate to Basil?
MARIE: Yeah, I don't know.
NORMAN: How did she choose him?
MARIE: I still don't know.

> *She slides the folder back.*

When did you lose your virginity … where did you lose your virginity … how did you lose your virginity? Oh no, wait … [*Snapping her fingers*] Have you lost your virginity?
NORMAN: You think you're clever.
MARIE: I'm clearly the most intelligent person in this room.
NORMAN: And threatened by me.
MARIE: Threatened? Pickle, I think you're delicious. In your world, you might imagine we're in some kind of conflict, you might even fantasise that you've made a solid point or two, but in the real world … and it is *lovely* here … [*Darkening*] Nothing you say matters.
NORMAN: Does it not?
MARIE: You can't make me lose faith in my son.

> *Standoff.*

> NORMAN *changes his strategy …*

NORMAN: If he wasn't groomed, if none of this was calculated, then how can you explain their relationship?
MARIE: Personal growth.

> *Spotlight:* BASIL *packs his bags.*

That's why I gave him the boot. I'm not a monster. [*Reassessing*] Not without reason.
NORMAN: You threw him out for his own good?

BASIL *takes a sad look at his room, and walks away to find a new life. The spotlight fades.*

MARIE: [*nodding*] But he didn't change all by himself.

NORMAN *smiles grimly.*

NORMAN: Ah, yes. The accomplice.

He licks a gloved finger, opens the folder, and turns a fresh page. 'The Only Way is Up' by Yazz marks another shift in time ...

SCENE NINE

Hairspray is the first thing we notice, wafting around a man in a towel ... ROGER THE KNOB *is back.*

The coffin has been taken away, but if we thought there were a lot of flowers at the funeral, things have just ramped up. This is a botanist's wet dream.

BASIL *enters, laden with suitcases. He has a newspaper tucked under one arm and whips it out to study intently, dropping his cases and sinking into one of the coloured beanbags that passes for a couch in* ROGER'*s pad.*

ROGER *mimes into his comb.*

Oblivious, BASIL *settles back into the beanbag. He doesn't even notice when* ROGER *moonwalks out of the room and his towel flies back, to land centre stage.*

BASIL *takes a pen from his top pocket and circles an article.*

ROGER *returns, in a dressing-gown—lilac, of course—and flips up two slices of toast, buttering them with a flourish.*

The room continues to transform ... the stage mechanics are transparent, but secondary to ROGER'*s dancing.*

BASIL *opens wide as* ROGER *shoves toast in his mouth. A* SNOOP *gives him a glass of orange juice.* BASIL *accepts it without noticing where it came from.*

More hairspray. ROGER'*s style is somewhere between Elvis Presley and Pauline Hanson. He receives a clock from a* SNOOP *and admires it. When a bar fridge is wheeled in, he openly high-fives the rest of the* SNOOPS, *too elated to take proper stock of them.*

The music reaches its chorus.

As BASIL *remains ignorant,* ROGER *dances with the* SNOOPS. *They love him.*

A kettle boils.

Normality returns.

Pause.

BASIL: I don't understand this Fred Basset.

> *He holds up the newspaper.*

ROGER: [*glancing down*] He fell off the monkey bars. That's it. That's his journey.

BASIL: But … what does it mean?

ROGER: It's Basset, not Beckett.

> *The* SNOOPS *accept cups of tea and coffee as* ROGER *pours. They leave with smiles, and maybe some Tim Tams.*

BASIL: Thanks for letting me move in, Roger.

ROGER: What are strained acquaintances for?

> ROGER *hands* BASIL *a cup, then moves a suitcase aside.*

BASIL: *Careful!*

> *The case shakes a little as* BASIL *unzips it and removes a small box … dotted with plenty of holes, and at least one conspicuous claw mark.*

My bearded dragon. Señor Pancake.

ROGER: House-trained, I assume?

BASIL: Yeah, but bitey.

> *He sets the box down.*

ROGER: Mind the chrysanthemums.

BASIL: The what?

ROGER: Purple bunch. On your right. Your *right.*

BASIL: Got it. [*Forcing a smile*] You're really making a go of this whole family business.

ROGER: Floristry isn't a 'business', it's a calling.

BASIL: Sure.

> *Beat.*

I meant to say, how nice they were.

ROGER: How nice …?

BASIL: The flowers.

ROGER: Ah.

Independently, they each decide to take an interest in their cups.

BASIL: Oh, and the eulogy, of course. That was … haunting.

ROGER: I'm uncomfortable with churches, Basil.

BASIL: Certainly came across.

ROGER: Did it?

Two of the loudest, most impolite—surprisingly competitive—coffee slurps. ROGER *sniffs.*

BASIL *shuffles.*

I'd like you to read some Dawkins.

BASIL: [*quickly*] I'm not … Mum and I, we're not … We just wanted to give him a good send-off.

They slurp again. Torturous pause.

Look, Roger, this shouldn't be for too lo—

ROGER: You never said anything.

Beat.

BASIL: …

ROGER: I know a divorce isn't the same as … But, you could have …

BASIL: No, no, I wanted to.

ROGER: Truly?

BASIL: It's just that—

ROGER: You never liked—

BASIL: Never. [*Swallowing*] Well, I didn't *dislike*, more a—

ROGER: Personal clash?

BASIL: Fear. There was … a bit of fear.

He has said too much.

If I'm being … Well, she wasn't exactly … Come on.

ROGER *sighs.*

BASIL *backs up a step.*

ROGER: Fear?

BASIL: Terror.

They return to their cups.

I *am* sorry, mate. I'm a shit friend.

ROGER: …

BASIL: You've been alone ever since?

ROGER: Ever since.

BASIL: With the … purple …

BASIL *gestures to the flowers.*

ROGER: Chrysanthemums.

BASIL: Chrysanthemums, yeah.

ROGER: Yeah.

ROGER *touches his incredible hair, soothing himself.*

She's with my delivery man now. Simian sex pest.

BASIL: He can't be that—

ROGER: It's like some hobo blew his wad in a bin, in Hackham, and nine months later that piece of shit crawled out.

BASIL *chokes on his coffee.*

BASIL: Well, I'm sure they'll be very miserable together.

No response at first, but slowly ROGER *brightens. He drains his cup.*

ROGER: You're damn right, Barry.

He raids the fruit bowl.

Water. Bridge. Banana. Moving on!

BASIL *catches an apple, just in time.*

So, what will a pair of eligible, *virile* boys-about-town do with their long and libidinous nights? Shall we noose ourselves some womenfolk?

BASIL: I don't … That's … No, mate.

ROGER: We're not boys though, are we? We're *men!*

ROGER *pounds his chest and peels his banana aggressively.*

BASIL: This really has been hard on you, hasn't it, Roger?

The banana munching gets a little despondent.

ROGER: Love can kick you in the sack, Barry. [*Refocussing*] But we can rekindle our bond.

BASIL: Our bond?

ROGER: We don't need anyone else to complete us. Together, we're a swollen force … a machismo train!

He belly-flops into a vacant beanbag.

BASIL: That's exciting, but … Roger …

Lost in his fantasy, ROGER *has started doing the breaststroke.*

ROGER: Picture it, Barry! Two spunk-torpedoes, armed and engorged, soaring towards those sweet, quivering—

BASIL: I need to tell you—

ROGER: And when the explosion comes—

BASIL: *Roger!*

Beat.

This isn't you, mate. You're not a 'machismo' guy, you're a … moscato guy.

ROGER *rolls onto his back.*

ROGER: It's never too late to reinvent yourself.

BASIL: You're a Devorak guy!

ROGER: [*correcting him*] Dvořák.

BASIL: See!

ROGER: Barbarian.

BASIL: That's the spirit!

A grunt, then …

ROGER: There's peel on my robe.

BASIL: I'll make it better.

He fetches a tea towel, moistens it and gently scrubs ROGER*'s dressing-gown.*

[*Soothingly*] You like concertos and petticoats, and olives with their pips removed.

ROGER: Pits. *Pits*. That's why they call them *pitted* olives.

BASIL: You like Campari. You're the only one, but you like it.

ROGER: Hmm, you know me too well, Barry. Baz. Basil darling.

BASIL: And there's something I'm *trying* to share with you.

He wipes ROGER*'s mouth clean.*

I met someone. Last night.

ROGER: You met …?

BASIL: Someone.

ROGER: Someone female?

BASIL: She was just—

ROGER: You met someone at your father's—?

BASIL: *She was just there, Roger.*

> *Beat.*

You saw her too. Dancing.

ROGER: With us?

BASIL: With me.

> BASIL *returns the tea towel to the sink.*

ROGER: And you … spoke to her? *You?*

BASIL: She whispered in my ear, and after that … I can't put it into words …

ROGER: You can try, my little Casanova.

BASIL: It's not like that.

ROGER: My horny Mark Antony.

BASIL: *Look out! Goldfish!*

> *Flustered,* BASIL *shoots in and retrieves one of his suitcases, mere seconds before* ROGER *rests his feet on it.*

We need to keep them apart. There's history there.

> BASIL *retrieves an aquarium, wrapped in tissue paper, and gently sets it down … far from his lizard box.*

> ROGER *checks the next suitcase, before making himself comfortable.*

ROGER: Try the balcony. Shift the cactus. [*With a deep sigh*] I can't believe you met a woman. At a funeral. That's … very gothic.

BASIL: I can't explain any of it.

ROGER: Tell me more, as Kenickie would say. I don't understand where this mysterious minx even came from. Did she know your father?

BASIL: No, she worked there.

ROGER: A mortician? Ghoulish.

BASIL: A caterer.

ROGER: Even worse! [*Damningly*] Did you try the blancmange?

BASIL: She got me out.

ROGER: [*thrown*] Out?

BASIL: Outside. Out of my head. Just, out.

> BASIL *can't meet* ROGER*'s eye.*

We kissed. In the rain.

ROGER: [*with a massive smile*] *'Holy Saint Francis, what a change is here!'*

BASIL: Don't think I'm easy.

ROGER: People never do that, Basil. Porn stars do that. DiCaprio does that, but actual, mortal humans—

BASIL: I need your help.

> *This brings a sparkle to the man in lilac.*

ROGER: [*hungrily*] Do you now?

BASIL: She's not like me, Roger. She's like … well, kinda like …

> ROGER *frowns.*

> BASIL *passes the newspaper over.*

This is her. I did a bit of … research.

ROGER: Stalking.

BASIL: *Research.*

ROGER: It's standard, don't worry.

BASIL: She chained herself to a blue gum.

ROGER: [*nodding*] And several friends.

BASIL: At first, I thought it was—

ROGER: A sex thing.

BASIL: What?

ROGER: But, alas, she appears to be—

BASIL: Political.

ROGER: Scary. [*Passing it back*] For you.

> BASIL *pulls up a beanbag, sliding close to* ROGER.

BASIL: That's my point. I don't get this stuff. I'm a …

ROGER: Dickhead?

BASIL: No, the other thing.

ROGER: Luddite?

BASIL: *Yeah!*

ROGER: And you want yours truly, the divorcé, the cuckold, to be your wingman.

BASIL: I don't need a 'wingman'.

ROGER: No?

BASIL: I don't need an ape with a banana in his gob.

ROGER: You're sure?

BASIL: I need *you*. The *real* you. [*Pleading*] I need the Roger who goes mental over apostrophes, the Roger who looks down on people who wear Crocs.

ROGER *plays hard to get, examining his nails.*

ROGER: So, instead of reinventing my wounded self, I'm supposed to reinvent you? That's a hard pass. Sorry, kiddo.

BASIL: I have money.

ROGER: [*scoffing*] You don't.

BASIL: I'll work for you. Deliveries. Front counter. Singing to the …

ROGER: Chrysanthemums.

BASIL: Those guys! *Every morning!*

ROGER *stands.*

ROGER: It's a challenge, Basil. I believe in your lust, but until now you've always been …

BASIL: Conservative?

ROGER: Hardly.

BASIL: A conscientious objector?

ROGER: Blank.

BASIL: Blank?

BASIL *is stung.*

ROGER: Well, there's not much going on upstairs, is there?

ROGER *points to* BASIL*'s brain. He might even tap it.*

That room has been vacant for years.

BASIL: …

ROGER: You've never engaged with anything real.

BASIL: …

ROGER: What's the name of our president?

BASIL: [*light bulb*] I think it might be—

ROGER: Trick question, dingus.

They both heave a sigh.

BASIL: Mum was right. I've just been taking up space.

ROGER: It will take a lot more than a gorgeous stranger to—

BASIL: I know that. It *should* take more.

> *Beat.*

But, she's one hell of a motivator.

> *A long, critical stare from* ROGER ...

> *He finally blinks.*

ROGER: And so, Pinocchio wants a seat at the table.

BASIL: I'll follow your lead.

ROGER: You shall.

BASIL: Question time. Electric cars. I'll learn to love it all.

ROGER: If you want to be real, you must start by opening those sleepy eyes of yours. Take a look at the wider world.

> *He claps his hand onto* BASIL*'s shoulder, lifting him from his beanbag.*

I'm going to make you perfect.

> *A wink.*

I'm going to make you me.

> BASIL *flinches.*

BASIL: That's thoughtful, mate, but … I—I think it's a radical interpretation …

ROGER: Skinny jeans.

BASIL: …

ROGER: We'll start with skinny jeans.

> *Lights fade.*

SCENE TEN

Darkness.

Flickering.

Scratchy footage. Black and white. Familiar to many … 'I Go To Sleep' by Sia rises.

We're in a tiny flat, marked only by a record player, the film projector, a swag and a few meagre belongings.

DELIA *curls up in front of the movie. She's watched this more than a hundred times.*

It's a Tasmanian tiger. The last one. 1933. Benjamin.

This film represents everything DELIA *hates in the world.*

She rolls up her swag. It's time to pack—conveniently enough, we have suitcases lying around.

SNOOPS *close in.*

They watch her zip up her cases; her sadness choked deep down in her chest, into a heart you don't want to fuck with. She has no time for tears, or to pick at scars.

And she has more than clothes to pack ... Boltcutters. Handcuffs.

Everything she's gonna need.

With one eye on the image, she takes out a pair of clippers, kneels down ... and hacks away at her hair, leaving it in black thickets around her knees. What's left doesn't quite reach her shoulders. It's messy. Uncivilised. As she has chosen to be.

She approaches the wall and touches the phantom tiger. Intimidated, the SNOOPS *literally fall away as she passes between them.*

Finally, she turns and taps the record needle. Silence.

Until ...

BASIL *appears, in spotlight.*

DELIA: [*a whisper*] I've been watching you.

> *Benjamin curls up in the corner of his cage.*
>
> *And flickers away.*

SCENE ELEVEN

Cheerful, and well-lit, once more.

ROGER, *prouder than ever, grinning like Garfield—and still wearing his dressing-gown—pontificates to a sherry in his hand.*

ROGER: One does not simply evolve overnight, but much as the butterfly emerges from her chrysalid, give me twenty-one days and I shall make you ... *informed.*

> *He feeds the fish.*

[*Scattering crumbs*] You've been locked within yourself, lacking intellectual nourishment. *I* will be that nourishment, Basil.

His eyes turn to the lizard box.

I bring life from listlessness, verve from ennui.

A little frightened, he drops kale and sliced fruit into the shuddering box, before letting out an Oscar-worthy screech.

God, it's a snake with claws.

He touches his heart, and downs his sherry.

BASIL: [*offstage*] I look like a dipstick, Roger.
ROGER: [*recovering*] Change is painful. But, you must slither out of that skin.

Peeping back into the box, gagging ... ROGER *daintily picks up his watering can and tends to his flowerbeds.*

Let your new self, the fresh flesh, materialise ...

BASIL *enters. Skinny jeans. Polo shirt. A sweater tied around his neck. This isn't him.*

BASIL: This isn't me.
ROGER: *Attends! La pièce de résistance!*

ROGER *snaps his fingers. A* SNOOP *plonks a beret onto* BASIL's *head.*

BASIL *shoots a glance back at the retreating figure, a silent question on his face ... 'Who the hell is that guy?'*

ROGER *takes command of his attention.*

Now, behold, like Mary Shelley, like Pygmalion himself, I have created ... No, this isn't you.

He deflates.

You look like—
BASIL: Marcel Marceau?
ROGER: A child killer.

BASIL *removes the beret.*

Still, this is cosmetic, what really counts is that you've *obviously* studied.

He thrusts some hefty books into BASIL.

Marceau. Beuchat. Abramović. Guðmundsdóttir. Powerful artists will stir the sage inside. Then, of course, the great thinkers …
BASIL: My arms can't take them.
ROGER: Marx. Confucius. Foucault.
BASIL: *Roger.*
ROGER: Bowie.
BASIL: *Jesus.*

Knees buckling, BASIL *dumps the books on a beanbag.*

ROGER: And the orators! Pericles. Churchill. Roosevelt …

BASIL *cowers as* ROGER *showers him with more colossal texts.*

… Mandela. Barry O. Clinton One and Two.
BASIL: How do you expect me to cram all this? I only have one brain.
ROGER: You've been lost in a fog, Bazza!
BASIL: It's not even a very good brain.
ROGER: *You're misty!*
BASIL: I'm average.

Beat.

Slightly below.

ROGER *collects more books from obliging* SNOOPS.

ROGER: Think of what you could accomplish if all that cerebral real estate wasn't choked up with … What *do* you think about?
BASIL: …
ROGER: And there it is.
BASIL: No, wait …
ROGER: Blank.
BASIL: I like Peter Jackson. [*Pouting*] And chicken nuggets.
ROGER: Fantastic. Human evolution has reached its zenith.

Beat.

There's a world out here, Basil. A world with consequence.

He throws the last of the tomes onto the beanbag.

Know your enemy.
BASIL: [*reading covers*] *Mein Kampf. The Art of the Deal.*
ROGER: Read this lot when you have nothing better to do.

BASIL: That day will never come.

> BASIL *drops them.*

I know you're trying to improve me, Roger ... but, I can't take in the whole world.

ROGER: Twaddle. You lack fortitude. Nothing else is holding you back!

BASIL: Start small.

ROGER: Domestic politics?

BASIL: Smaller.

ROGER: Cake forks?

BASIL: A little more ambitious.

> ROGER *slips into a meditative pause. He regards his flowers, cogs turning.*

ROGER: Picture yourself at a garden party.

BASIL: What do you mean?

ROGER: A party in a garden.

BASIL: Yes.

ROGER: [*miming*] Cravat. Boutonnière. Moscato.

BASIL: And where is—?

ROGER: Forget your filly ... you must fit in first.

BASIL: Who am I fitting in with?

ROGER: Our people.

BASIL: Our people?

ROGER: No, *our* people. Hers and mine.

BASIL: You're very different.

ROGER: Political people, Basil dear. *Relevant* people.

BASIL: She's stronger than you.

ROGER: To us, the popular is rancid, the rancid is chic, Bob Hawke governs Olympus and *Q&A* is sacred time. We appreciate the subtle flavours in fermented grapes, the whimsical side of communism, and ...

BASIL: Leigh Sales?

ROGER: Leigh Sales. Excellent.

BASIL: I just get my news from Facebook.

> ROGER *swats him.*

ROGER: Facebook isn't news, my wet philistine. I could go on Facebook tomorrow and say, 'The sun is a giant omelette' ... if Alex Jones hasn't already.

Beat.

Now, repeat.

BASIL: [*imitating him*] Cravat. Boutonnière. Moscato.

ROGER: This feta is heavenly.

BASIL: This feta is heavenly.

ROGER: Gillard was robbed.

BASIL: Gillard was robbed.

ROGER: My eldest lives in London.

BASIL: My eldest lives in—

The doorbell rings.

ROGER: Blast. If it's the Mormons, you'll fetch my hose. Or my pruning shears.

BASIL *runs to the window.*

BASIL: *It's my mother!*

ROGER: In that case, we'll require a shovel.

BASIL: Turn off the lights. We'll hide.

ROGER: Now, now, this could be fortuitous, Baz … we do need a practical test.

BASIL: Mate, I haven't even passed the oral exam. [*Looking down*] She's going to laugh at me.

ROGER: Is she capable of laughter?

The doorbell rings again.

BASIL: She can't come in if she's not invited.

ROGER: [*rolling his eyes*] Try putting the cashmere around your waist.

ROGER *sprays his hair, before preening himself in the mirror … that is really a toaster.*

BASIL: Do I look *that* bad?

ROGER: Like someone who decorates in baby skin.

BASIL *throws the sweater away and undoes his top button.*

BASIL: Understood. Not accepted, but understood.

He opens the door.

Hello!

MARIE *strides in, passing shopping bags to her son—no sign of the sling.*

She's wearing dark glasses and a headscarf. Audrey Hepburn meets The Fly.

MARIE: I brought coffee. Good coffee.

ROGER: We have coffee, Marie.

MARIE: You have instant.

BASIL: Mum.

MARIE: Like someone shat in a jar.

BASIL: *Mum.*

ROGER: You look well.

MARIE: [*to* BASIL] There's toothpaste and toilet paper … you always go overboard with that … and I collected those …

BASIL: *Orcs!*

Devastated, BASIL *riffles through the bag. He withdraws some orc pieces.*

You've killed them.

MARIE: I'm turning your room into a library. [*Noticing the books*] Have you been reading too?

MARIE *removes her glasses, picks up a book and arches an eyebrow.*

ROGER: That's … for research purposes.

MARIE: *Inside the Third Reich.* Well, better than *Playboy.*

ROGER: Not really.

MARIE: [*brushing* ROGER *aside*] You'll come for the rest of your belongings, won't you, Basil?

BASIL: [*re: the orcs*] What did these poor guys ever do to you?

MARIE: Basil. Don't bore me.

BASIL: Yes, alright, I'll come over and wipe my childhood away.

MARIE: Have you cut your hair? It's awful.

ROGER: He styled it.

MARIE: I asked you a question.

ROGER: Have I evaporated?

BASIL: I'm trying some new things, Mum.

MARIE: Stupid.

ROGER: *Marie.*

A scary beat.

MARIE turns, balefully, to regard ROGER.

It's … really special to have you in my home.

MARIE: How was your divorce, Roger?

ROGER: Tough. [*Looking away*] I haven't been very …

MARIE: No? Shame.

ROGER: Shame.

MARIE: [*a smile*] Coffee?

BASIL shoots ROGER a sympathetic look, as ROGER—gutted— busies himself with the kettle.

BASIL: What do you think of the flowers, Mum? We've got purple, bit of yellow.

MARIE: Reminds me of the Botanic Gardens.

ROGER: That's the idea.

MARIE: Zombies in wheelchairs. Teen mothers with needy children.

BASIL: You can't say—

MARIE: Oh, welcome to Earth, Basil. [*Turning to ROGER*] If he gets any more flaccid on your watch, I'll express my disappointment with bleach and vinegar.

She strokes the chrysanthemums. ROGER dies inside.

For a long time, I was worried that my child would be a sharper version of me. I read that baby sharks eat their siblings in utero. But I needn't have fretted. [*Arctic*] There's a lot of Howie in him.

BASIL: [*with a thin smile*] Well, thanks for the toothpaste.

MARIE: The mechanic left you a bill. I can't believe you made me google 'rim job', I saw some very disturbing acts … and not nearly enough tyres.

BASIL: Is this fridge honey or cupboard honey?

MARIE: It's the same honey, Basil.

Checking ROGER for confirmation, and getting a sad nod in return, BASIL takes the honey and the rest of the shopping upstage.

My editor mentioned you as well. He said he saw you, after the funeral.

BASIL freezes.

BASIL: He … saw me?

MARIE: Running. In the rain.

> *She's onto them ...*

> BASIL *looks at* ROGER. ROGER *looks at* BASIL. *DEFCON 2. Battle stations.*

ROGER: [*sliding in*] It's not as weird as it would appear.
MARIE: New haircut ...
BASIL: *Style.*
MARIE: ... hipster duds ... brow wax ... [*Sniffing*] ... Dior.
BASIL: I always use—
MARIE: You use Lynx. Like a thirteen-year-old.
ROGER: It's an experiment.
MARIE: Or an attempt to impress someone.
BASIL: Maybe, but Roger says I remind him of—
MARIE: Hitler Youth.
BASIL: [*appalled*] No, a child molester.
ROGER: Killer. [*To* MARIE] I said *killer*.
MARIE: [*needling*] Someone who paints figurines in his bedroom.
BASIL: I do paint figurines in my / bedroom.
MARIE: [*over him*] Have you joined a / cult?
ROGER: [*over her*] *We're not Nazis, Marie.*
MARIE: ...

> *That didn't go well.*

> ROGER *moderates his tone.*

ROGER: [*carefully*] I'm trying to educate your son.
BASIL: *Dude.*
ROGER: Not in a fascist way! I'm teaching him what to avoid and what to ... project.
MARIE: [*to* BASIL] Who's the girl?

> *Beat.*

BASIL: Delia. Her name is Delia.

> *The kettle boils.*

> MARIE *saunters over to it, leaving* ROGER *to mouth a heartfelt 'sorry' to* BASIL. *Everyone takes a moment to find their footing ...*

> MARIE *gets there first.*

MARIE: *Playboy* was the first thing he ever read independently. I knew then, my son would never be a scholar.

She pours herself a cup.

His first girlfriend had to go to ICU. He bit off a third of her tongue. An even third. Imagine. [*To* BASIL] Digested it, didn't you?

ROGER, *subtly, tries not to retch.*

Enthusiastic, my boy … but, never bright … never intellectually curious. [*Smiling*] Sugar?

BASIL *and* ROGER *both point to the sugar bowl.*

None of this peacocking is necessary. Making a connection is simple. Talk about your dog. Talk about her dog. Talk about the parallel lives of these dogs.

ROGER: He doesn't have a dog … he has a velociraptor.

The lizard box wobbles.

MARIE *keeps her gaze on her son.*

BASIL *senses that his mother is up to something …*

MARIE: Women spend decades, whole marriages, trying to change the men in their lives. You're doing it for her, before your first date. How very—

BASIL: Progressive?

MARIE: Spineless.

She stirs her coffee, claiming centre stage.

I've finished the actual homework on this one. Delia is not your kind of girl.

BASIL: You don't get to decide.

MARIE: I'm clearly the most intelligent person in this room.

She sips.

Any room.

The energy has shifted. ROGER, *destabilised, senses that he has been left a few exits behind.*

ROGER: Baz, why do I feel like the temperature has dropped in here?

BASIL: [*to* MARIE] You're not going to ruin this.

MARIE: [*scrutinising* BASIL] They want to know what she whispered to
    you … what made you chase her out, into the rain …
ROGER: Who wants to know?
MARIE: The people.
ROGER: *What people?*
BASIL: The people who are watching her.

SCENE TWELVE

Red lights.

'A Victory of Love' by Alphaville on maximum volume …

Unsettling. In a synth-pop way.

*Not quite a Rubik's cube of colour this time, the stage has become a
chequerboard of crimson squares.*

Downstage left, DELIA *is a dark angel in sniper black. She wipes her
face clean, leaving smears of dirt and blood on a lilywhite handkerchief.
Silently, she chides herself: 'Get it together, bitch'.*

Downstage right, BASIL *tapes a microphone to his bare chest and
inserts an earpiece. His face says a lot too: 'Is this really my life now?!'*

DELIA *unzips her blacks.* BASIL *buttons his shirt.*

DELIA *slips into a floral muu-muu. Hyde becomes Jekyll.*

BASIL *slides into a Tom Ford jacket. Weasley becomes Bond.*

DELIA *regards her reflection, practising coquettish smiles.*

BASIL *checks his notes. Memorising lines. It's now or never.*

*Both spin, synchronously, and head upstage where … a scoreboard
flashes.*

The music is drowned by the clatter of falling pins.

DELIA: Strike!
BASIL: That was a lucky—
DELIA: *Strike.* Accept it, Peppercorn! Your arse is so whipped.

    Lights up. Bright and safe.

    *Video games whirl in the background, and kids wail, but it's the
    clatter that tells us where we are.*

BASIL: Bowling is for plumper men.

DELIA: Aww, is the thrice-time loser a bit sore? How are those glutes?

BASIL: My … derrière is just fine, thank you.

He bowls. Badly.

DELIA: We should have gone with the gutters. I didn't believe you when you said you sucked.

BASIL: I never said—

DELIA: Thought you were being humble but, you're really, *really* medium at this.

She brushes him aside. He watches her bend over. Catches himself.

Looks away.

Another satisfying clatter.

BASIL: That one was already wobbly.

DELIA *straightens.*

DELIA: Admit you've been outmatched. Purge yourself.

She throws him a smug grin.

BASIL: [*falling hard*] Of what? My chivalry? I don't have anything to prove here.

DELIA: Yet you've proven so much.

BASIL: …

DELIA: Poor motor skills.

BASIL: Debatable.

DELIA: Pissweak hand-eye coordination.

BASIL: Vicious.

DELIA: A butt worth kicking.

BASIL *freezes as* DELIA *invades his personal space.*

BASIL: Handsy.

DELIA: Alcohol.

She leads him downstage, to where the lights have turned green. Abruptly, they're mid-bender:

BASIL: I don't think it's that hilarious.

DELIA: [*in paroxysms of laugher*] She named you after a culinary herb.

She tastes her phrase. Savours it.

[*Over-enunciating*] Culinary. Herb. That's you.

She downs her glass.

BASIL: Seems you're getting a little dizzy there, Delia Dongle.

He snatches the beer nuts.

DELIA: Dengel.

She snatches them back.

BASIL: Dengel.

He takes a fistful.

DELIA: Enjoy your salty E. coli.

BASIL: I shall. Delia.

DELIA: Fuck you, I'm named after a moon goddess.

BASIL: Is that right?

DELIA: Goddess of the Hunt. [*Pointing*] I'm up there ruling the universe, you're down here in the unpopular square of the salad bar.

BASIL: [*scandalised*] *The unpopular square?*

DELIA: With the lemon wedges, and the scungy pesto.

She pushes the nuts out of his reach.

I'm saving your life.

Beat.

BASIL: Salmonella.

DELIA: …?

BASIL: It's more likely to be salmonella than E. coli. [*Off her stare*] E. coli mostly comes from beef.

DELIA: [*correcting him*] Dead cows.

BASIL: Pardon?

DELIA: You said 'beef', but you're talking about dead cows. It's like when people say 'economical' instead of stingy, or 'freelancer' instead of unemployed.

BASIL: Guess that makes me a freelancer.

He raises his glass in a self-pitying salute.

DELIA: There are heaps of them. 'Artistic' instead of boring. 'Conservative' instead of fascist. People are so—

BASIL: You're a person, Delia.

Beat.

DELIA: Wish there was a way I could opt-out.

The vibe has spun into melancholy. BASIL *slaps the bar.*

BASIL: Another round of your finest moscato.

DELIA: Is that what this shit is? [*Laughing*] It's like wine for Teletubbies.

Relieved to have drawn a smile from her again, BASIL *turns and waves some cash at …*

NORMAN GOULD. *Trying to be a barman.*

He's a little too neat and overdressed by inner-city standards; a little too much like Lloyd from The Shining.

NORMAN: Perhaps the lady would enjoy a jammy shiraz?

DELIA: [*smiling*] The lady has a pulse, so why don't you ask her?

NORMAN: I'm sor—

DELIA: Mai Tai. No, wait … Flaming Lamborghini.

She ruffles BASIL*'s hair.*

For me and the gentleman.

His cover in jeopardy, NORMAN *squirms, open-mouthed.*

NORMAN: Are you sure you wouldn't prefer a gin and tonic?

DELIA: That's funny.

DELIA *walks away.*

BASIL: Where are you—?

DELIA: Gonna rub one out in the bathroom. Take the edge off.

She exits.

Pause.

BASIL: [*to* NORMAN] She's probably just urinating.

NORMAN: Very good, sir.

BASIL: It's our first date.

NORMAN *folds a napkin into a rectangle and dabs his forehead.*

NORMAN: Two Flaming …

BASIL: [*prompting*] Lamborghinis.

NORMAN: Two Flaming Lamborghinis.

BASIL: If it's no trouble.

NORMAN: No trouble, no. Two Flaming Lamborghinis. [*Pepping himself up*] You've got this.

BASIL *watches* NORMAN *leave. If he wasn't so love-struck, he may sense something amiss. Instead, he reaches for the nuts ...*

A pitchy squeal.

BASIL *clutches his ear.*

BASIL: *Arrgh!*

He tears the earpiece away.

ROGER: [*offstage*] Higgins to Doolittle ... Higgins to Doolittle ...

ROGER *enters, stupendously dressed. Purple suit. Matching homburg. Give him a cane, if you like.*

Come in, Doolittle!

He is screeching into a microphone, oblivious to the pain he's causing.

BASIL: *I'm here, Roger.*
ROGER: You fell off the map, Barry. What happened?
BASIL: She took me bowling. [*Deadpan*] That's the crisis.
ROGER: I was concerned, so I thought I'd slip over. Incognito.

Beat.

BASIL: This *is* discreet for you, isn't it?
ROGER: I didn't want you to feel marooned. We're sexual partners!
BASIL: ...
ROGER: In crime!
BASIL: That's not better.
ROGER: I'm the Carraway to your Gatsby, the Brandybuck to your Took.
BASIL: Sit down.

ROGER *does as he's told. Then ...*

ROGER: [*beaming*] Tumtum to your Nutmeg.
BASIL: *Quietly.*

NORMAN *returns. The cocktail has baffled him. He mixes spirits with an increasing sense of panic, his façade cracking.*

NORMAN: [*with forced cheer*] Is this your first Flaming Lamborghini, sir?
BASIL: Yup.
NORMAN: [*relieved*] Wonderful.

He draws a blowtorch.

But you might want to stand back.

BASIL: [*concerned*] You've used this before, haven't you …?

NORMAN: [*a flash of malevolence*] Not for burning cocktails.

ROGER: Barkeep. [*Sauntering over*] One Ramos Gin Fizz, *s'il vous plaît.*

Beat.

NORMAN: Remind me.

ROGER: Freshly squeezed lemon juice, freshly squeezed lime juice, sugar syrup, vanilla extract, gin …

NORMAN: Slower.

ROGER: … an egg white …

NORMAN: [*to* BASIL, *earnestly*] Is this a cake?

ROGER: … orange blossom water and precisely two tablespoons of … Where did I lose you?

NORMAN: Lime juice.

ROGER: Scrub it out. I'll have an Old Fashioned.

NORMAN: An old-fashioned what?

ROGER: [*erupting*] Bourbon, a dash of bitters, a maraschino cherry … *Why do I feel like I'm adrift among the nomadic tribes of thirteenth-century Mongolia?!*

He tears some notes from his money clip and smacks them onto the bar.

BASIL: I'm sorry, um …

NORMAN: [*gracefully*] Vermouth, sir. Artemis Vermouth.

ROGER: Oh, my apologies, it's nineteen seventy-six and we're all extras in a continental porno. [*Staring* NORMAN *down*] Whiskey. Neat. That means if you add ice, you *shall* be garrotted.

BASIL: Don't take your nerves out on—

ROGER: That's not a whiskey glass, that's a Seidel.

NORMAN *tries again.*

That's a flute. Not to worry, I hear Colonel Sanders is hiring.

BASIL *exhales.*

BASIL: I shouldn't have agreed to this. Did I agree to this? You coerced me.

ROGER: You *asked* me to coerce you.

BASIL: I asked you to teach me, not tie me in strings.

ROGER: You wheedled.

BASIL: Fine, I wheedled. But we're getting along. Why can't I just be …
myself?

ROGER: No, no, that's the last thing you want to be.

BASIL: If we manipulate her, how are we any better than—?

ROGER: We're *always* better. [*To* NORMAN] That's a vase, you saddle-
goose.

BASIL: Roger, this isn't fair on her.

ROGER: Trust the process, Basil.

BASIL: I want to do this honestly.

A door opens.

BASIL: She's coming back. Be natural.

ROGER: Be—

BASIL: Natural. Normal. *Pretend.*

ROGER *backs away from the bar and adopts an affected pose.
It's not natural, or normal.*

What the fuck is that?

ROGER: I don't know, Basil.

DELIA *returns.*

ROGER *dives into the nearest chair. She glances over at him. He
plays dead.*

NORMAN *straightens.*

NORMAN: Won't be a jiffy, madam.

DELIA: Better call a cab for Grimace over there.

NORMAN: Indeed.

NORMAN *exits.*

DELIA *slides her stool over to* BASIL.

DELIA: You look anxious.

BASIL: [*quickly*] No!

DELIA: …

BASIL: Defensive.

DELIA: And what does one do to break down those defences?

She touches his thigh.

BASIL: It'd probably take a small army. A helicopter. A good one. [*Looking down at her massaging fingers*] Maybe a s-sss-submarine.

DELIA: Make love, not war.

BASIL: You're such a hippie.

> BASIL *gently takes her hand in his.*

DELIA: Third generation. I'm a flower grandchild.

BASIL: I'd never have guessed.

DELIA: Gran and I used to hand out copies of *The Big Issue* on Grote Street. Afterwards we'd get—

BASIL: Ice cream?

DELIA: Salad.

> DELIA *withdraws her hand. Pointedly.*

BASIL: I used to spend my weekends dusting.

> *Beat.*

My mother is Beelzebub.

DELIA: [*with a smile*] No, she isn't.

BASIL: [*with a sigh*] No, she isn't.

> DELIA*'s hand rests on the bar.* BASIL *places his hand on top of hers. There is a moment of tension.*

Now, *you* look / worried.

DELIA: Do you know where the word 'hippie' comes from? It's West African, it means to 'open one's eyes'.

BASIL: I didn't know that.

DELIA: So, when you call me a hippie, what you really mean is … I'm awake.

BASIL: I'm awake too.

> DELIA *laughs. There is no humour in it.*

I *am.*

> *Her smile wilts into a scowl.*

DELIA: [*studying him*] You think you make your own decisions? Cute.

BASIL: …

DELIA: Start calling things what they are, Basil. Life will be a lot less grey.

> BASIL *senses the hurt in her.*

She gently falls back into his chest, and turns her head up towards him.

He leans in to kiss her ...

There is an explosion from the kitchen.

NORMAN *appears. His face is blackened, his eyebrows singed. He may be swatting out smoke, or stray flame.*

Everyone stares at him.

NORMAN: [*desperately professional*] The shiraz has a full, fruity, baked-apple finish.

The spell has been broken ...

DELIA *and* BASIL *consciously uncouple.*

DELIA: [*pissed*] Show me.

NORMAN *trails after* DELIA, *as she strides away.*

ROGER *gestures for* BASIL *to reinsert his earpiece.*

ROGER: [*into the mic*] How are you faring?

BASIL *speaks into his lapel.*

BASIL: The theory hasn't prepared me for the prac. She is *tough*, Roger. Amazon tough.

ROGER: I think she looks quite ... bloomy.

BASIL: She's a Goddess of the Hunt.

ROGER *hops back to his feet and risks a look offstage, studying their target.*

ROGER: A whiff of sass is *de rigueur* for the modern progressive, but I assure you my advice *always* wins out. Order the osso buco.

He hands BASIL *a menu.*

BASIL: It's veal.

ROGER: It's cultured.

BASIL: It's dead calf.

DELIA *is back. She has a bottle in hand, and* NORMAN *at her heel.*

DELIA: Do you want to get out of here? Artie says this one is on the house. [*Turning*] I heard you right, didn't I, Artie?

NORMAN: Well, no.

DELIA: [*to* BASIL] Artie will get over it.

BASIL: You sure you don't want to stay and eat some osso …?

> *He looks back at* ROGER.
>
> *Falters.*
>
> ROGER*'s eyes widen; Cecil B. DeMille watching his actor dry on stage.*

I mean … you probably wouldn't like …

> DELIA *places the bottle on the bar, waiting for* BASIL *to find his voice box.*

[*Light bulb*] Gillard was robbed.

DELIA: What? When?

BASIL: [*the bulb breaks*] I … don't know.

DELIA: That woman has been through so much.

> BASIL *shrivels. He can't keep this up anymore.*

BASIL: Listen, Delia, you're right about me, I don't make my own—

DELIA: You don't say.

> BASIL *feels the power shift. He would like to connect with her, to find equal footing … but* DELIA *has found the menu.*

[*Reading*] Dead baby sheep, dead baby goat, ooh, here's a good one … *foie gras.*

BASIL: I need to tell you this.

ROGER: [*under his breath*] Abort, Basil, abort.

> DELIA *draws closer to* BASIL. *She suddenly takes him by the throat. It's intimate, and loving … then brutal as hell.*

DELIA: That's when they grab a duck, stick a tube down its neck, and force-feed it three times a day, to fatten its liver. When the duck can hardly walk, and the liver is *eight times* its normal size, you've reached the pinnacle of style and sophistication. [*With a hollow laugh*] Delectable, am I right, Artie?

NORMAN: …

DELIA: [*back to* BASIL] Did you watch Donald Duck when you were a kid, babe?

BASIL: …

DELIA: Aw, not easy to swallow with my hand around your neck, is it? [*Treacly*] Ask the lady again if she's feeling peckish.

She lets him go.

BASIL: [*rubbing his throat*] That ... sounds ... very cruel.

DELIA: Does it? Glad I'm capturing the nuance.

BASIL *forces some lightness into his tone.*

BASIL: [*playfully*] But you can't eat salad all the time, if you do that you'll be wea—

DELIA *grabs* BASIL, *turns him and pins him against the bar.*

ROGER *moves to intervene—or to look like he wants to—but* NORMAN *remains frozen.*

Perhaps intrigued. Perhaps vindicated.

DELIA: [*to* BASIL] Do you think I'm a moron? That I haven't been under surveillance for *most of my adult life*?

BASIL: It's not what you think. My friend was ... helping me.

DELIA: I'm awake, Basil. I know my own mind. I'm confident. I'm clever. [*Into the mic*] And I don't agree with you.

ROGER *clutches his earpiece. He lets out a wail.*

The jig is up.

DELIA *relaxes her grip on* BASIL ... *but she still holds onto him.*

BASIL: We're not with the government, or anything like that. Roger is just giving me some subtle pointers.

DELIA: Subtle? The guy who looks like Kelsey Grammer knocked up Truman Capote?

ROGER: Gutter banter. How droll.

He straightens his creases.

You're not one of us, Delia.

DELIA: Are you two aware that we have portable phones now? With buttons? You could've texted each other like sensible gangbangers.

BASIL: We weren't stalking you. I promise. This is *fear*, not cruelty.

DELIA: You never know who might be watching.

NORMAN *stands upstage of* BASIL *and* DELIA, *silently drinking in the scene ... with the faintest smile.*

ROGER: [*taking control*] Step away from her, Baz. She's unhinged.

DELIA: Almost like I'm an activist. A real one.

ROGER: He doesn't need to be muddied by the likes of you.

> *Beat.*

DELIA: Make a decision.

> BASIL *reaches down and picks up the bottle.* DELIA *is still holding him.*
>
> *He carefully plucks her hand away. She gives him a disappointed frown. But then ...*

BASIL: [*in a whisper*] I want to get out of here.

> *His hand tightens around hers. She grins.*
>
> *And they're running.*

ROGER: Basil, wait …

BASIL: [*over his shoulder*] See you round, Artie!

> *They exit.*
>
> ROGER *throws up his arms in exasperation, before screwing up his homburg and pouting his way out the door.*
>
> *Pause.*

NORMAN: Until then …

> NORMAN *grabs a fistful of beer nuts.*

Mr Pepper.

SCENE THIRTEEN

That summer storm is brewing, once again. Lightning flickers in the distance, followed by thunder's warm purr.

DELIA *leads* BASIL *back to her flat.*

BASIL: That was incredible. I feel like—

DELIA: Oliver Twist?

BASIL: *Batman!*

> *Beat.*

DELIA: Batman saved Gotham. Repeatedly. You just ran away.

BASIL: Fine. I'm Oliver Twist. That's Green Arrow, right?

DELIA: That's Oliver Queen.

BASIL: Well, then who's—?

She kisses him.

DELIA: [*gently*] Don't expect a medal. You're not awake yet.

A grin.

You're still dozing.

BASIL *is left stunned and horny, while* DELIA *starts gathering her suitcases. Pause.*

BASIL: I smoked a joint once.

DELIA *raises her eyebrows.*

[*Correcting himself*] Held a joint. Didn't inhale.

DELIA: And now you pay taxes, like a good boy.

BASIL: Um, no, I don't make any money.

DELIA: Everyone gets broken in.

She unzips a case, throws in a torch and what looks suspiciously like a switchblade ... her eyes lingering with something like guilt; something like hunger.

They allow for a little rebellion. Teen drinking, maybe some premarital orgies ... but, in the long game, they trust us to grow up. Put out the bins. Conform.

BASIL *digests this.*

BASIL: Mum doesn't want me talking to you. She thinks—

DELIA: It's not me she's afraid of. She's heard the rumours.

BASIL: She's seen the *pictures*, Delia. Protests. Brawls. You're lucky / you've never been hurt.

DELIA: Lucky to be born in a time when I can *do* something.

BASIL: Is it any wonder that you're being wa—?

He corrects himself again.

That you're under surveillance?

DELIA *flicks her blade. Studies it. Appreciates it.*

DELIA: What did you imagine my life to be?

BASIL: Garden parties and moscato.

> *Beat.*

> DELIA *erupts. This is the funniest thing she's heard in a long time.* BASIL *keeps his eyes on the blade.*

[*Warily*] Roger taught me to project a sense of … connection with the world.

> DELIA *is abruptly stone-faced.*

DELIA: He taught you to lie?
BASIL: No.

> *Shadows cut through the venetian slats and slice the space between them. Each time the lightning strikes, the room feels sharper… stranger …*

> *The eye of the storm is focussed on this house. This couple. Rain hammers.*

I want to do better. I can. If you'll help me.

> DELIA *approaches* BASIL *… and uses the blade to cut through his shirt. Stifled gasps. Popping buttons.*

DELIA: I've met many people like your buddy Roger. People who make all the right noises, but never leave their chairs.

> *She brings the blade up to tap* BASIL'*s nose. It's playful, and just this side of psychotic.*

> *Merrily so.*

The sort of people who buy a KeepCup for their Nissan Armada. They'll say, 'We're overpopulated', but they *love* their grandkids.

> BASIL *is relieved to watch her put the switchblade away, but confused when she slides another suitcase over to him.*

My favourites are the ones who lecture about climate change around their family barbeques. [*Gesturing*] Open it.

> BASIL *looks down at the case.*

The beef industry smacks the oil industry down when it comes to environmental fuck-ups. Forget ExxonMobil. Forget Shell. Forget BP. Look on your plates, dickheads.

The suitcase is full of black clothing. BASIL *takes it out.*

Put those on.

BASIL: …

DELIA *rolls her eyes at his modesty, and wriggles out of her dress.*

DELIA: Methane, land grabs … Actually, the water use alone is enough to make every other environmental cause meaningless. But, sure, sign some petitions, Roger. Make a difference. Nighty-night.

Mimicking her, BASIL *dresses in the blacks.* DELIA *admires him.*

You look good.

Beat.

BASIL: Dead cow industry. [*Off her frown*] You said 'beef', but it's …

DELIA: [*a real smile*] Dead cow industry.

She takes his hand again.

I care. I don't want to be *seen* to care. I actually, genuinely, give a fuck.

Her hand reaches past him, to touch her film projector. Their lips are close.

[*Intimately*] But this world is broken.

The projector sputters to life.

DELIA *checks her watch and finishes her inventory.* BASIL *is left to gaze up at the image.*

BASIL: I've seen this. The last Tasmanian / tiger.

DELIA: [*razor-sharp*] His name is Benjamin.

Beat.

He survived for three years. Pawing at walls.

BASIL: I guess he was waiting for …

He loses his smile, and shrugs sadly.

Just, waiting. [*Turning away*] I … can't imagine being the last of my kind.

DELIA: I can.

That's the final case to check. DELIA *heaves a sigh. Steels herself. Murders the last of her doubts.*

BASIL *watches her back.*

BASIL: I let the mice go.

DELIA: …

BASIL: In biology class. Year Eight. I let the mice go. Mum yelled at me. Sent me to my room without supper … which was great, because it was her shitty chilli and … and … You know, I think Dad was proud. He *looked* proud.

He swallows.

Why me?

DELIA: …

BASIL: Why did you choose me, Delia?

A moment's hesitation. DELIA *doesn't trust easily.*

BASIL *takes a step closer to her, freezing when she speaks …*

DELIA: Because of what you said. At the funeral.

BASIL: I didn't say anything at the funeral. I sat there being cowardly. Being blank.

DELIA: You said everything after the service. When you thought only your dad was listening. I heard you … [*Turning to face him*] I watched you.

Beat.

BASIL: Dad loved his garden. Even when we moved to the city, he set up flowerboxes and aquariums. He taught me to respect every living creature. Lizards were as cute as kittens to him.

He grins at the memory.

And then to me.

DELIA *stands and shuts off the projector. Between the venetian slats are new shadows—*SNOOPS*—closing in, circling, watching.*

DELIA: I lost someone too.

BASIL: [*unsettled*] Is *that* why you were there? Do you … troll funerals?

She brightens.

DELIA: Maybe.

And, when she turns, she's loading a pistol. BASIL *freaks.*

BASIL: *Delia!*

DELIA: Ssh, it's your initiation, Basil. Like letting the mice go, but ... a little more public. This is Plan C. [*With a shrug*] It's licensed, if that helps.

> *She flicks the safety lock.*

The knife is Plan B.

BASIL: I feel sick.

DELIA: Plan for the world as it is, hope for a better one.

BASIL: And what's Plan A?

DELIA: Persuasion.

> *The pistol looks comfortable in her steady hand ... But she has no intention of holding onto it.*

Don't look at me like you don't understand. I know you do.

BASIL: ...

DELIA: I used to think, 'Fuck it, I'll go into politics one day'. Now I think, 'Fuck it, I wanna go down swinging'.

> BASIL *finds his voice.*

BASIL: *You keep a gun in your flat?!*

DELIA: Oh, babe ... this isn't my flat.

> *Lightning.*

> DELIA *holds the weapon out to* BASIL.

> *The thunder is much closer now, and louder.*

Tell me more about your dad.

BASIL: He'd say ... h-hello to everyone. [*Raising his hand*] He'd look after even the f-f-feral animals. Pigeons. Rats. We had a fox for a while.

> *He accepts her gift, muzzle to the floor.*

DELIA: It's time you honoured him.

> *She smears black stripes under her eyes, like an Amazon ... like a tiger.*

> *She moves around* BASIL, *their bodies never breaking away.*

[*Into* BASIL*'s ear*] I don't want you to change yourself. I want you to *be* yourself.

> *Music rises, competing with the storm. This time, it's gonna win.*

The shadows stretch.

Identical coats.

Identical hats.

We're alone, but we're together. Two of a kind.

BASIL *lifts the pistol. Steadies his hands. Savours the weight of it.*

They're all around us. Judging us. Stomping us down.

She guides his arm up.

I'm not talking about the government. I'm talking about the apathetic. The faceless cowards.

They're here now ...

SNOOPS. *More than we've ever seen. They close in around the lovers.*

Spectral. Anonymous. Menacing.

They cage us because they fear us.

BASIL*'s aim is sure. He's pointing straight ahead. Straight into the audience.*

Anyone who's anyone is on their list.

The music kicks up, as rain cascades ...

END ACT ONE

'On their cattle plague feeds, on their tilth feeds frost, and the old men cut their hair in mourning over their sons, and their wives either are smitten or die in childbirth …'

Callimachus of Cyrene

ACT TWO

BELONGING

SCENE ONE

Darkness.

Thunder.

Electricity.

An iconic drum launch ...

'Bizarre Love Triangle' by New Order bursts into being.

Downstage left, DELIA *appears, virtually unrecognisable. She has become a corporate darling, all pinstripes and high heels.*

Downstage right, MARIE *is doing her best Billy Blanks impersonation. She has splashed out on active wear.*

DELIA *slicks her wild curls down.*

MARIE *boxes the dickweeds in her mind.*

They turn, synchronously, and head upstage, to be replaced by ...

Downstage left, BASIL *crouches in full commando regalia. Tight black T-shirt. Flak jacket. Camo pants. His jaw is set.*

Downstage right, ROGER *stares miserably into the horizon. He wears that same lilac dressing-gown. It hasn't been washed in months.*

BASIL *draws a hammer and a set of tree spikes. Grins to himself.*

ROGER *pours brandy into his coffee. Takes a liberal swig.*

They turn, synchronously, and head upstage, to be replaced by...

A sparkle of colour.

A silhouette. A hard hat.

*Centre stage, the figure—*NORMAN GOULD—*shakes in time with the synths. One bare thigh stomps rhythmically.*

As the lights turn, he spins to face us. Denim shorts. Shredded singlet. Tool belt. He went for butch and landed on David Hodo. Of course, his expression remains as stern and professional as ever ...

He whips out a wrench.

The music climaxes.

ROGER *sinks into a beanbag. The spell breaks.*

He turns over, scattering TV snacks. Sounds of midday television ...

Snatches of dialogue. Soapie themes.

NORMAN *has moved to the sink, where* MARIE *glowers. It's just the three of them now.*

MARIE: You're not worried? Not even a smidge?

ROGER: Dick Van Dyke has such a dirty name.

MARIE: *Roger.*

ROGER: He abandoned us, Marie. How long do you expect me to pine for that ninnyhammer?

MARIE: He can't take care of himself.

ROGER: It's high time he practised. *Infernal cub.*

> *He waves the remote control. Sounds of an AFL match.*

> MARIE *moves over to him. She holds two plastic cups of fresh green puke.*

MARIE: Here. It'll help with the hangover.

ROGER: I don't have a—

> *But as* ROGER *sits up, his head turns against him.*

Argh. God. Bury me now.

MARIE: It's wheatgrass.

ROGER: I prefer bourbon.

MARIE: Are you really trying to negotiate with me, Roger?

> *Checkmate.*

> ROGER *accepts the puke.*

ROGER: I'd get more warmth from Saddam Hussein.

MARIE: He's dead.

ROGER: Precisely.

> MARIE *pulls up a beanbag.*

MARIE: This isn't going to help us.

ROGER: I'm not trying to ease this crisis, Marie. I intend to flounder.

MARIE: He needs a—

ROGER: Bosom companion? Oh no, all evidence to the conflicting. I've been scrapped. Forsaken. *Again.*

Sighs from both.

MARIE: Well, perhaps, you need—

ROGER: I don't need anyone. It's just my excellent self, these Cheezels, and Bruce McAvaney!

MARIE backs up as ...

ROGER pulls himself to his feet and towers over her.

Bruce is a simple man. We'll be very, *very* average together.

He downs the glass. Brings most of it up.

Damn you.

Pause.

MARIE: Is he still paying rent?

ROGER: What's with the unitard? Are you training for Noosa?

MARIE: Answer my—

ROGER: *You first.*

MARIE: Fitness.

ROGER: You're a bowling lady ... if you can bend your hip, you're playing at an elite level.

MARIE: My husband is dead.

This freezes ROGER.

Heart attack, remember?

ROGER: [*thawing*] Of course, I remem—

MARIE: Good. [*Shaming him*] Strangely, that whole event left an impression.

ROGER: I'm sorry, I was daft.

MARIE: Does my son owe you any money?

ROGER: …

MARIE: I'll fix it up.

She stands.

ROGER: No.

Beat.

I'm terrified for him.

MARIE: Me too.

A momentary understanding.

I rejected him, didn't I?

ROGER: You kicked him out of your nest and into mine. This all happened on *my* watch. That … vapid hyena picked him off while I had my nose in the air.

He turns away. Wistful and steamy-eyed.

You placed your trust in me and I failed.

MARIE *scoffs.*

MARIE: I never placed my trust in …

She corrects her course.

I will find it in my heart to forgive you, Roger.

Beat.

Now, for pity's sake, rinse something.

ROGER *sniffs his arms.*

ROGER: I've been stinkier.

MARIE: You smell like egg and you look like Elvis.

ROGER: [*elated*] Do I?

MARIE: Right before he had a cardiac arrest on the toilet.

MARIE *resumes her exercises.*

ROGER: Well, I haven't had a chance to—

NORMAN: *Here's your problem!*

They both turn and take NORMAN *in. He wanders over, hitching his tool belt.*

Washer split. You're running a high temperature. [*To* ROGER] Do you ever come out pink after a long bath?

ROGER *recoils into his dressing-gown.*

ROGER: That's a very private image.

MARIE: I don't think he's bathed since the Kennedy assassination.

NORMAN: You find this a lot in these old buildings. A regulator will save you, in the long run. I'll cut you a deal.

NORMAN *tips his hard hat to* MARIE *and exits.*

MARIE: You're having some plumbing done?

ROGER: The whole building needs an upgrade. They're fixing the wires too.

MARIE: Fixing the wires?

> *Before* ROGER *can elaborate, the AFL commentary is replaced by a breaking news theme.*

VOICE: *Coming up: Pastoralists in the Echunga region have reported damage to agricultural equipment, after tense encounters with ...*

MARIE: Where's the remote?

ROGER: There's plenty of time.

VOICE: *... claims of fences slashed, and livestock set free ...*

MARIE: I want to hear this.

ROGER: It's coming up!

> *They search the beanbags for the missing remote.*

VOICE: *... similar concerns have been raised about the upcoming Oakbank Racing Carnival ...*

> ROGER *finds the remote.* MARIE *pounces.*

ROGER: You're hurting my arm, Marie.

MARIE: Ssh. I want to hear.

ROGER: It's coming up.

MARIE: Roger, be quiet.

ROGER: It's coming up! It's *coming up*!

VOICE: *... the federal government has announced a crackdown ...*

MARIE: That's him!

> *They both freeze.*

That's my Basil.

ROGER: Christ, he's coming up ... Basil is coming up ...

MARIE: Did he witness something?

> ROGER *grabs his Cheezels.*

VOICE: *The new Swivel Sweeper will revolutionise your breakfast nook.*

MARIE: Shove your Swivel Sweeper up your—

ROGER: *Basil!*

MARIE: *No!*

NORMAN: I can get you better reception.

Behind them, NORMAN *has returned, with power cables coiled around his shoulder.*

MARIE: It's not him.

ROGER: It's *so* him.

NORMAN: It's a cinch … the antenna is pointing the wrong way …

ROGER: This is *incredible!*

NORMAN: … it won't take me long to twirl it around …

MARIE: How could he do this?

NORMAN: It's those bloody river gums.

MARIE: To me?

ROGER: *Astounding!*

MARIE: To *my* life?

NORMAN: Do you have a ladder handy?

> ROGER *abandons all words …*
>
> *He stuffs his face, his chin and most of his neck with Cheezels.*
>
> *Together,* ROGER *and* MARIE *sink into a beanbag.*

VOICE: *Authorities believe this was a premeditated act …*

MARIE: I should've pushed harder for that beagle.

VOICE: *… causing thousands of dollars in property damage …*

MARIE: Tied my tubes.

VOICE: *… lost earnings …*

MARIE: Snuck in a dental dam.

> NORMAN *joins them, munching Cheezels. A tense beat.*

VOICE: *We're crossing live to the farmers now.*

> ROGER *empties Cheezel dust down his gullet.*

MARIE: I'm not going to get angry.

VOICE: *Police are searching for this young man.*

MARIE: I'll kill him.

> *Blackout.*

SCENE TWO

The shadowy flat.

DELIA *is holding up more corporate outfits—suits, blazers, sensible shawls—all with tags still attached, and all very un-Delia.*

Her eyes glower into darkness, and mirror glass beyond. She is tightly coiled.

BASIL *enters, chewing gum. He drops envelopes as he walks.*

BASIL: Owners are in London. [*Reading*] Mr and Mrs Limos. Lucky ducks. They must be loaded if they're not even bothering to rent this place out.

> *He pops a bubble.*

> *Booya!* BMW. BM *fucking* W! [*Looking up*] Are you going to an arraignment?

> DELIA *doesn't turn.*

Delia?

> *It takes a second for* DELIA *to leave her thoughts behind and acknowledge* BASIL. *He was teasing her, but his smile has already fallen away.*

DELIA: Were you seen?

BASIL: [*unsettled*] Nah, I just … emptied the letterbox. It was piling up and the neighbours were … well, I don't know if they were *looking*, really … but … better to be safe than … Seriously, do you have to dress like my mother?

DELIA: Lock the door. Now.

BASIL: I have.

DELIA: Check.

BASIL: It's bolted.

> *He stands his ground.*

> [*Re: the envelopes*] Vet bills. Couple of Dalmatians. That explains the fur in—

DELIA: You're too comfortable.

> *The intensity in* DELIA*'s gaze doesn't waver. She drops the clothes in a heap, crosses past* BASIL, *and touches the door.*

BASIL: We don't deserve dogs.

DELIA: [*to herself*] We don't deserve any of them.

> *She turns back to face her lover. Sees him examining the pile of clothes. Straightens. Sighs out her anxiety. And performs.*

[*Upbeat*] So, why aren't you slobbering on me? It *worked*. You staged your first protest. Made them feel it.

BASIL: I know.

DELIA: Hurry up and be / happy.

BASIL: What's in the suitcases?

DELIA *shifts into one of her well-practised, coquettish smiles.*

I deserve to know everything. Where you go. Why you lie.

DELIA: [*a quiet warning*] Don't try to cage me, Basil.

BASIL: I see these outfits. Your corporate skin. You have me messing with farmers, while you—

DELIA: You don't want to know what I do. What I *must* do.

BASIL: Open it. [*Turning*] Open all of them.

She doesn't move.

Was my mother right? Are you / dangerous?

DELIA: I'm a terrorist. Call things what they are.

BASIL *tears through the cases, scattering clothes and cuffs, and ... photographs.*

He picks them up. Gasps.

Were you expecting a bomb?

BASIL *pushes the images away.* DELIA *approaches him.*

[*Gently*] I smile my way through bolted doors. I see things we're not supposed to see, and I share them.

BASIL: ...

DELIA: I spread terror. The terror we allow. [*Hopeful*] Sometimes it helps. Sometimes someone cares.

Beat.

Sometimes.

She waits for him to relax.

Not all heroes wear capes, Howie.

Faint thunder.

Not all villains wear masks.

Spotlight: NORMAN *throws his hard hat aside, and reaches for his trilby.*

BASIL *backs away. Anxious.*

DELIA *opens her arms. Eager.*

BASIL: Howie? That's my—

DELIA: Dance with me, babe.

She doesn't wait for his consent—instead, she flicks the needle on her record player and draws him into her stare.

'Raspberry Swirl' by Tori Amos hits hard. Manic. Feverish. The sort of song that belongs at four a.m.

DELIA *appraises* BASIL.

She doesn't really want to dance.

She wants to distract him. To own him.

He smiles uncertainly, even as she presses her body against his.

She turns her back to him, coaxing his hands around her snaking form.

BASIL: Lashing out, then pulling me in …

Red lights rise.

[*Flippantly*] You're acting like a psychopath.

A sly smile lands on DELIA. *She turns until her face is hovering close to* BASIL*'s, their noses brushing.*

DELIA: You think *this* part is the act?

It's a joke. Probably.

The music drives their pounding heartbeats. Just as he's about to kiss her …

She breaks away and becomes a silhouette.

Spotlight: NORMAN *turns and summons the* SNOOPS. *The whole stage is red now. A bloody mist.*

The SNOOPS *close in.*

BASIL *is passed from one pair of gloved hands to another. They slap dirt across his cheeks, smear him in engine oil, and spatter him in gravel or grit, or gore.*

DELIA *dances.*

SCENE THREE

Twilight at the bins.

ROGER *enters, cardboard box tucked under his arm. He begins separating the hard and soft plastics.*

BASIL: You're wasting your time.

> *A yelp from* ROGER. BASIL *appears, in shadow.*

Recycling is deeply hypocritical after a steak dinner.

> *It takes a second for* ROGER *to compose himself. He finds his snark.*

ROGER: Ah, brilliant. Lurking in the street like Dickensian riffraff! Is this the new Barry?!

BASIL: You tell me, friend.

> ROGER *squints.*
>
> *The figure that steps into the half-light is not the* BASIL *we know. He's seen some shit.*
>
> ROGER *takes in the camo pants, now torn, and the splatter across his cheek—part oil, part shingle, part blood. But it's the new confidence in* BASIL*'s eyes that takes some getting used to.*

ROGER: [*recovering*] Well, it's a bold style. Ecotage chic.

> *He returns to his recycling, fastidiously inspecting each item.*

BASIL: The dead cow industry is choking the planet. I don't think taking the lids off your gravy tins is going to balance the scales, do you?

ROGER: I don't recall requesting an audit from the Animal Liberation Front.

> *Suddenly,* BASIL *has crossed the space between them. There's a weapon in his hand.*

Are you going to stake me?! Help! He's insane!

> BASIL *covers* ROGER*'s mouth.*

BASIL: It's a tree spike, Roger. Loggers hate them. They mess up their chainsaws. [*Laughing*] God, you're pathetic.

> *He lets* ROGER *go.*

ROGER: A tree spike. Is that … permissible?

BASIL: …

ROGER: Oh, I don't like this, Baz. I don't like *any* of this.

BASIL: You know, if we all ate the grain that we feed our livestock—

ROGER: We'd all be anaemic beatniks, with indigestion. [*Softening*] Please, mate, this isn't you.

BASIL: It is.

> BASIL *toys with the recycling.*

ROGER: She's a nymph, Basil. I'm the chum who gave you a chance. I treated you with gentility and respect / while—

BASIL: While you treated everyone else with disdain.

> *Beat.*

I'm not like you, Roger.

> *He takes a carton out of the box. Crushes it.*

> *A hostile pause.*

Funny that you think you're helping.

ROGER: [*hurt*] *Funny?*

BASIL: Like any of this makes a dent.

> *He bins the carton.*

Every time you stuff your face full of viscera, you're contributing to biodiversity loss, deforestation … even our resistance to antibiotics.

ROGER: Isn't that—?

BASIL: Nah, not a good thing. Not if you want to stay alive.

> *A flash of lightning.*

> BASIL *closes in on* ROGER.

I'm going to assume you don't give a fuck about animals, so consider this … mass farming produces more greenhouse gas emissions than cars, more than trains, more than every mode of transport combined. [*A mean smile*] Seems like the flower children have been picking on the wrong people, doesn't it?

> ROGER *tries to squirm away.* BASIL *holds him.*

One kilo of dead cow takes *fifteen thousand litres* of water, and more roughage than you've ever eaten. [*Quieter, fiercer*] We're raping the land and killing the climate, so we can call ourselves 'manly' and 'cultured'.

He picks up the recycling box.

This is a placebo. A bandaid on a heart attack.

The box rolls into the bin.

So, tell me ... seriously ... which one of us is insane?

Thunder.

ROGER: My, she has broken you in, hasn't she?
BASIL: Don't.

ROGER snatches the tree spike.

ROGER: Is *this* what makes a difference?
BASIL: [*ignoring him*] Cholesterol! Now, that's a fresh chapter ... you may as well butter your arteries and call them scones at this point.
ROGER: Does it help you feel powerful?
BASIL: It helps me feel *useful.*

BASIL reclaims his spike.

ROGER digs his box out of the garbage. His recycling becomes more insistent, cartons and cans aggressively sorted.

ROGER: Sanctimonious prick.
BASIL: Avaricious asshole.
ROGER: *I taught you this vocabulary.*

BASIL grabs some of ROGER's garbage.

BASIL: You're jealous because I've learned to walk the walk. All you do is drown your regrets, and wallow in—
ROGER: *Lean Cuisine! It's not like I'm harpooning whales!*

ROGER tears the garbage from BASIL's hands.

BASIL: You only know how to moan and condemn.
ROGER: *Stop groping my Ribena!*

They squabble until dogs bark and cats yowl.

A police siren passes in the distance.

Both freeze.

Come indoors.

BASIL: …

ROGER: You wouldn't be back here if you didn't need my help, Basil.

The siren is no longer fading—it's turning about, drawing nearer.

BASIL: They're circling the block.

ROGER *darts forward, grabs the spike, and banishes it to the bin.*
Hey!

ROGER: Leave it, you fool.

He takes hold of BASIL*'s hand and drags him upstage.*

SCENE FOUR

Lights up. The flat.

Red and blue beams flash beyond the window. Both duck until the car passes.

BASIL: Gone.

ROGER: For now.

BASIL: I just came back for my stuff.

ROGER: Who hurt you?

ROGER *reaches out.* BASIL *slaps his hand away.*

BASIL: This is the new normal.

ROGER: But who—?

BASIL: *People who kill things for a living.*

ROGER *flinches.*

Beat.

ROGER: Did you know you featured on three broadcasts? Leigh Sales
was talking about *you.*

BASIL: So what?

ROGER: So, while you've been rattling off SparkNotes about the ecology,
I've been saving your tuchus.

BASIL: Nobody can identify me.

ROGER: Your *mother* can identify you.

BASIL: She's not that vindictive.

ROGER: …

BASIL: Shit.

The car returns, siren blazing.

They crouch, hold their breath, and watch it whizz by. ROGER *starts chortling, in panic's grip ...*

What's wrong with you?

ROGER: Hysteria! No ... *schadenfreude!* Your catastrophes are my catnip!

BASIL *slaps him.*

ROGER *rolls over.*

BASIL: It's sad that you think you have the moral high ground.

ROGER: [*clutching his cheek*] *I'm not perfect, but at least I'm law-abiding!*

BASIL: Compared to you I'm *Mother Fucking Teresa!*

ROGER: I would've gone with Pope Francis, but if you're more comfortable comparing yourself to an old lady ...

BASIL: *Prince of Lies!*

BASIL *closes the window.*

ROGER: *Czar of Bullshit!*

ROGER *shuts the curtains.*

BASIL: Where do you get off?

ROGER: Where do *you* get off?

Then ...

[*Fresh horror*] The / door!

BASIL: [*stumbling over him*] The lamp!

They both run in opposite directions, taking each other down.

BASIL *rolls—literally, rolls—his way to the nearest light source. If it's a lamp, it's coming down with him.*

ROGER *crawls to the front door and latches it tight, but not before tipping the chrysanthemums.*

ROGER: *My beauties!*

The lizard box is next to fall. ROGER *shrieks as it shakes in his arms.*

BASIL: Don't scare / him!

ROGER: *Scare him?!*

> BASIL *snatches, and steadies, the box.* ROGER *falls back into a beanbag.*

> *They sit ... and wheeze.*

Why couldn't you have joined the RSPCA like a normal person?

> BASIL *lets out a sigh.*

BASIL: I'm sorry.

ROGER: No, *I'm* sorry.

BASIL: I'm still a shit friend.

ROGER: I was your Touchstone ... the Miss Honey to your Matilda.

> *Beat.*

We lost our compass, Basil. I failed you. Like I failed my marriage.

> BASIL *softens, if only a little. Some of his old patience returns.*

BASIL: Don't be like that. You're always surrounded by women who admire you.

ROGER: And yet I can never organise a three-way.

> *They both crack a smile.*

BASIL: The macho routine is still not a good fit, Roger.

ROGER: Stay here, Basil. Be ridiculous with me.

BASIL: …

ROGER: Be safe.

> BASIL *stands.*

BASIL: I've found my purpose. You can call it a 'catastrophe' if you want to.

ROGER: I was only teasing.

> BASIL *reaches into the flak jacket and withdraws a pair of handcuffs.*

> ROGER *stares.*

> BASIL *throws them to him.*

BASIL: I meant every word.

> *Blackout.*

> *A light bulb descends.*

SCENE FIVE

NORMAN: You knew we were watching her. Even before we brought you in.

> *The light bulb flickers to life.*

You knew weeks ago.

MARIE: There's a list. Every closing society has one.

> NORMAN—*suited and shadowy once more*—*paces downstage.* MARIE *is back in her pantsuit, her arm hanging in its sling.*
>
> *The tape recorder turns.*

A list of undesirables, of miscreants.

NORMAN: I'm not going to confirm—

MARIE: You don't have to confirm anything. I'm a swot from way back. I love the tricky homework. [*Rising*] These people have never been charged with a crime … many are flawlessly lawful, with not so much as a parking ticket … but still you list them. Delia knows she's on that list.

NORMAN: It's about security.

MARIE: Do you think so? [*Baiting him*] She has always been a step ahead of you, and I've always been a step ahead of … every other human.

> *A stare passes between them.* NORMAN *twists his into a smile.*

NORMAN: Closing society? How glib.

MARIE: When you're lumping activists with paedophiles, I'd say you're pretty close-minded.

NORMAN: *Manners, Ms Harbuck.*

> *He stalks back to her.*

I've a fox to flush out and your son is the—

MARIE: Beagle? Please say beagle. That would be destiny.

NORMAN: I could have him charged. Detained. We work without oversight.

> MARIE *gets up close to him. Close enough to kiss.*

MARIE: I enjoy you, Norm. I really enjoy you.

> *She grins.*

Tell me about the vintage recorder. Is that a funding issue? Or is Big Brother afraid of being watched?

NORMAN: Ah, that literary imagination.

MARIE: Bet you never pick your nose in front of your webcam.

NORMAN: Perhaps you should write thrillers, after all.

MARIE: Perhaps.

> *But she's got him, and she knows it.*

It's clever … in that proud, fascist tradition. Unlimited surveillance. Weaponised paranoia. If you make the enemy your own people, that war machine just keeps on chugging in the background. [*Quieter*] Why don't you do something happy with your life? Start a garden.

> NORMAN *chuckles.*

NORMAN: Interesting. You're not only protecting him.

> *He turns the bulb her way.*

You're protecting *her.*

> *Beat.*

MARIE: There aren't many people I admire, because the human race is largely horrible … but she's up there.

NORMAN: [*astonished*] Why?

MARIE: How many of us can say we really care about something? Beyond ourselves, our families … and the one or two pets we've deigned to love.

NORMAN: Jihadis care too. Do you want to send them a fruit basket?

> MARIE *groans.*

MARIE: *Come on, Norm.* Most of us have signed up for monotonous ephemera from nine till five. We've forgotten what it means to be hopeful. I mean, Jesus, is *this* who you thought you'd be when you were young?

> *She takes the bulb. Turns it back on him.*

Was Norman Gould born without empathy?

> *A withering beat …* NORMAN *bites his lower lip.*

> *It takes a few seconds for him to defrost, but* MARIE *isn't blinking.*

NORMAN: I used to keep snails. Garden snails.

> *He waits for* MARIE *to laugh. She doesn't.*

I hated the sound they made … the crunch when we trudged up the driveway. My brothers thought it was hilarious. They'd go out of their way to … [*Swallowing*] And then we'd fight. And my parents would ask why. And I'd be ashamed.

MARIE: …

NORMAN: Do you remember Gus the Snail? I used to watch him, every afternoon. He'd have a little television on his back, or a flowerpot.

MARIE: I remember.

NORMAN: The voice was marvellous. He sounded like old-school Australiana, like a granddad with crinkly eyes and a crooked smile. People went to him for advice … or, sometimes, a knock-knock joke.

> *Beat.*

I never had anyone like that.

MARIE: [*gently*] How many did you save?

NORMAN: Dozens. I named them all. Fed them carefully. I even re-searched it, back in the time when children went to libraries. Then winter turned, and my brothers moved their tank too close to the window. The summer heat … [*Hardening*] Kids are pitiful. We grow up. We wipe our noses. We get our priorities in order.

MARIE: Do we?

NORMAN: They were *snails*, Ms Harbuck. Nobody ever wept for—

MARIE: Liar.

> *She savours the crack in her captor's façade.*

So, there it is. I admire Delia because she's humane, and we are … like you said … too grown up for that.

> *She resumes her seat.*

> NORMAN *waves a dismissive hand … but the memories are stirring now …*

NORMAN: When I was young, I imagined I could put my hand through the television screen and touch a better world.

> *He looks at his glove.*

A *kinder* world. Where everyone, and everything, would be safe.

> *The hand drops.*

There's a price to be paid for a world like that.

MARIE: Not our compassion. Not our trust. That's too high.

NORMAN: …

MARIE: Poor Norm. You started from a kind place.

NORMAN: They were too slow to have any chance. It wasn't fair.

>   *Beat.*

  It wasn't justice.

MARIE: My son is slow too.

NORMAN: No. [*Darkening*] Not if he's chasing her.

>   *Rain falls.*

SCENE SIX

A bed.

A spinning record.

'Every Breath You Take' by Denmark + Winter, ghostly and bittersweet, plays.

The storm makes the shutters rattle, and turns shards of moonlight into a spectral mosaic of liquid shimmer and phantom hailstones. It's all consciously surreal; the way a first, forbidden love lands.

BASIL *returns. Still filthy. Still torn.* DELIA *beckons to him.*

He moves to her side.

She dips a cloth in warm water and tenderly wipes the dirt—the damage—away. From all around, SNOOPS *gather to survey them.*

The lights shift.

And so does the room ...

The SNOOPS *form a circle, gently turning the bed, rotating 360 degrees, while* DELIA *purifies* BASIL.

There is something sacred about this act. Something primitive. Ritualistic. When his face is clean, she moves to his hands, his arms, his upper body ... Finally, she draws her knife. Holds his gaze. Slits her palm, and then his.

He flinches as she presses their wounds tight; their fingers clenching, interlacing. The SNOOPS *peel back into the ether.*

DELIA *lays* BASIL *down, kisses his forehead, and then rises ...*

Spotlight: MARIE, *in her active wear, a world away.*

The two women look down at their hands: DELIA *at the fresh red line;* MARIE *at the fading scar.*

Both turn to regard BASIL. *Longing—and regret—stain their faces. They watch him.*

SCENE SEVEN

A tangerine glow. We're on the roof of Roger's building, where ravens mix with car horns.

Handcuffed to the fire escape, ROGER *himself is not enjoying the chilly open air.*

ROGER: [*calling*] Help! Bloody ... heeeeelp!
NORMAN: Hello?
ROGER: Heeeeeeeeeeeeeeelp!
NORMAN: *Hello?*

> NORMAN *wanders in, holding an antenna. He is dressed in his skimpy shorts, tool belt and hard hat. Back in character.*
>
> *He nods, pleasantly.*

You alright there, skip?
ROGER: ...
NORMAN: I'm having trouble getting the commercial stations. And the other ones.

> *He plants the antenna. Fusses with it.*
>
> ROGER *stares.*
>
> *Beat.*
>
> *Eyes still on the antenna,* NORMAN *settles down, takes out his lunchbox and tucks into a little tub of yoghurt.*

Nice up here, eh?

> *He licks his spoon clean. Sighs.*
>
> *Adjusts the antenna. Sits back down.*
>
> ROGER *clears his throat.* NORMAN *offers him the tub.*

ROGER: *Look at me, you slack-jawed loitersack!* Do you think I'm sitting on the roof for leisure?! I'm cuffed to the fucking fire escape! *My testicles are snow cones!*

NORMAN: What happened, mate?

ROGER: *Hacksaw!*

NORMAN: Come again?

ROGER: Get me a—

NORMAN: Hacksaw won't cut through those. Too dull.

ROGER: *Blast!*

NORMAN: Should cut through bone, easily enough. [*Grinning*] Which hand?

ROGER: Staywhereyouare! [*Calling*] *Help! Heeeeeeeeeeeeeeeeeeeelp!*

NORMAN: Easy, Princess.

> *He slips a pin into the cuffs. They snap open.*

ROGER: I'm not amused.

> *But* NORMAN *is.*

> ROGER *shakes the blood back into his hands.*

Was there anyone downstairs?

> NORMAN *inclines his head. The act drops.*

NORMAN: [*eyeing him*] You're expecting someone?

> *Beat.*

ROGER: Take the rest of the day off. I think I'll stay up here. Enjoy the stars.

NORMAN: Are you sure that's—?

ROGER: My chums and I play pranks. Have a lark. Pull the old chain. [*Pointing*] I'll tell you what …

> *He returns to his cuffed position.*

Why don't I set myself up for some top-shelf payback? As they return, I'll pounce.

NORMAN: Is it safe?

ROGER: Perfectly.

NORMAN: Mate, if you're in any kind of trouble, say 'sparrowhawk'. [*Deadly serious*] It's a Eurasian bird.

ROGER: I'm fine.

NORMAN: No sparrowhawk?

ROGER: No sparrowhawk.

NORMAN: …

ROGER: Skies are clear.

Pacified, for the time being, NORMAN *heads for the exit.*

I'll see you in the morrow!

Giggles rise.

ROGER *twists himself back into his former position. Convincingly cuffed.*

DELIA *and* BASIL *appear. She is back in black. He is now wearing his plush chameleon costume. They fool around—high on each other—before she peels his hood away and kisses him.*

DELIA: When you said you had the perfect disguise, I was imagining something less ... Basil.

BASIL: A chameleon *is* the perfect disguise. Check me out. Ha! You *can't.* I'm blending in. [*Off her smile*] My uncle has a reptile house. I was his mascot for two sad summers.

DELIA: We're not staying long. Feed and water your flatmate, then we'll—

BASIL: Five minutes.

He takes her by the hand and leads her to the roof's edge.

I climb here all the time. Usually at sunset, when the streetlights wake up.

DELIA *looks down at the road ...*

DELIA: Hello, tiny ant-people. [*Then up at the clouds*] Ooh, that's a Bell 412.

BASIL: Well spotted. I've always wanted to fly a chopper.

DELIA: Same.

BASIL: Da Vinci designed his own. The Aerial Screw.

DELIA: I've heard of that, but not in a design context.

BASIL: It took four men.

DELIA: Kinky.

They both laugh.

BASIL: We've got so much in common. [*Nodding, to* ROGER] She's a pottery fan too. Knows her way around chintzware.

ROGER *can barely conceal his disgust.*

ROGER: If it isn't the maniac and the microphallus. I was hoping you'd leave me for dead.

DELIA: That's so hurtful. [*To* BASIL] It's almost like he doesn't want to spend quality time with us.

ROGER: Basil, she may look like Nana Mouskouri ... but, on the inside, she's Charlie Manson.

DELIA: Don't wet yourself. We just need to stop you from—

ROGER: Going to the authorities? Reporting a break-in?

BASIL: I pay rent, Roger.

ROGER: Your mamma pays rent.

> DELIA *settles down beside* ROGER, *laying an arm over him.*

DELIA: So, you two go way back, hey? At school they called you ... [*To* BASIL] What was it, hon?

BASIL: Roger the Knob. Like Alexander the Great.

ROGER: [*turning away*] Well, he *was* great.

DELIA: [*pinching his cheeks*] Well, you *are* a knob.

BASIL: Come on, it doesn't have to be—

ROGER: It will always have to be like this. She's uncompromising.

DELIA: Yes, I am.

> *A savage beat.* ROGER *swallows.*

ROGER: Since we're doing nicknames, you two are quite the Bonnie and Clyde.

> DELIA *and* BASIL *share an adoring smile.*

That's not a recommendation. Some of those farms you hit were ethical.

DELIA: Ethical. Sure. Because naming an animal, teaching her to trust you before you open her throat ... that's positively angelic.

ROGER: I don't claim to agree with their—

DELIA: It makes the meat more tender when the animals are less stressed. [*Nudging him*] When you pretend to love them.

> *Beat.*

But, if you don't agree, then everything's *fine* ... isn't it, Roger?

> *When no reply comes,* DELIA *pats his head and returns to* BASIL.

BASIL: [*to* ROGER] You don't have to understand, or be part of this, but I do ask that you respect—

ROGER: Just do whatever you came to do and go.

> BASIL *nods.*

BASIL: [*to* DELIA] Watch him.

> DELIA *cracks a smile.* BASIL *exits.*
>
> *Silence ... save for the faint call of traffic, meandering below.*

DELIA: You have a nice view, Roger. Stars. Sky. Smog.

> *They look down at the city.*

ROGER: Why are you attacking their livelihoods? These are real people, Delia. Simple people trying to make ends meet.

DELIA: I'm sure they'll be touched by your arrogant concern. What about all the poverty *caused* by farming?

> *She turns back to face him.*

They're not feeding the world, they're hoarding resources.

ROGER: It's just us talking now. You're very far from stupid, so you know it's a system, a chain, and it's not the producers you're waging your war on. Those are the little guys.

DELIA: Spoken like an armchair Marxist.

ROGER: It's the contractors, the corporations ... ultimately, the consumers ... and unless you want to take down the human race ...

DELIA: I want to prove that we can change.

> *Beat.*

ROGER: We can. I believe that too. But, violent gestures / won't—

DELIA: Won't they?

ROGER: ...

DELIA: [*laughing*] Our planet is terminally ill. Revolutions have been fought for far less.

> *She leans down to him.*

I feel sorry for you, Roger. You don't believe in anything.

> BASIL *returns.*

BASIL: I'll take it from here.

> *An anxious pause.*
>
> DELIA *turns and raises her hands. The gesture is clear: 'I wasn't going to hurt him'.*

BASIL *tries to smile, but he's not completely convinced.*

DELIA *draws close to him. Kisses his cheek. Locks her eyes onto his.*

DELIA: Until tonight.

BASIL *nods.*

Don't let him scare you, Roger.

ROGER: Well, there are a lot of puppets in horror films.

DELIA *finds that genuinely funny—for about three seconds—before she flashes a cold stare* ROGER'*s way, clicks her tongue, and exits.*

BASIL *and* ROGER *take a breath to adjust to each other's company.*

That could be the police up there. Looking for you.

BASIL: Nah, that's a medical helicopter.

ROGER: Is it? Hmm.

He squints up at the sky.

If you *do* go to jail, you can get free food, and lodging. And sex.

BASIL: Nobody's going to jail.

ROGER: I wonder if she'd even visit you.

BASIL: *Shut up, Roger.*

Without his lover to support him, BASIL'*s resolve is rickety. He slams a backpack down between them.*

ROGER: It's plain to me you're hanging by a thread. [*Leaning forward, nastily*] Would you like to borrow my scissors?

BASIL: [*sweating*] I'm not above gagging you, alright?!

ROGER: What are you even looking for?

BASIL *pulls miscellaneous objects from the backpack: broken orcs, fish food, a couple of the recommended biographies, and finally ... a newspaper.*

BASIL: Fred Basset. Smug little prick.

He turns the paper around.

Oh God.

The paper falls from his hand.

Why didn't I see him before?

Suddenly, ROGER *is free and looming over him ...*

ROGER: See who?

BASIL: *Aaaarrgh!*

> *He scuttles away from* ROGER.
>
> *There is a brief scratch-up between them, but* ROGER *is more intent on barring the escape route.*

How did you get free?!

ROGER: Brain clobbers brawn, Barry. I've been stalling you ... [*turning*] ... on orders from High Command.

MARIE: Basil.

> MARIE *joins them on the roof. She's wearing the now iconic pantsuit and shawl, but her arm is fine—we're getting to that.*

You don't have to flip out. We're trying to help you.

BASIL: [*to* ROGER] You told her I was here?

ROGER: She has been here *every day* since you absconded.

MARIE: This is an intervention.

BASIL: She's supposed to be at book club.

MARIE: I gave up on book club. You can't drop the F-bomb. Quiches are shit.

> BASIL *makes a dash for the fire escape.* ROGER *nabs him.*

It's fine, Roger. He'll behave.

BASIL: This is not even child abuse anymore. It's just wanton violence.

MARIE: Let him go.

> ROGER *releases his grip.*

Is it true?

BASIL: Is what—?

MARIE: *Everything.*

> BASIL *looks away.*
>
> *The tension cools. A little.*

All I want for you is a steady job and a mainstream love interest. I suppose that's too much to—

BASIL: I want something bigger.

MARIE: How can this possibly end well for you, Basil? Think about it.

ROGER: You're asking for critical thought? May as well ask a cabbage to write a symphony.

MARIE: Blowhard.
ROGER: Harridan.
MARIE: *Sit!*

> ROGER *flops into a deckchair. He couldn't look more peevish if he rehearsed.*

> BASIL *finds a less adversarial tone, squeezing out the last of his patience.*

BASIL: I was trying to be independent. Obviously, I've failed again.

> *Pause.*

MARIE: I've told you three times this week, Basil …
BASIL: [*downtrodden*] Well, you know I generally need four.
MARIE: I love you.

> *Beat.*

BASIL: Why does everything have to be a competition between us?
MARIE: I like to win.

> *She keeps a straight face.*

But I *love* you.

> *The tension dissolves …*

> BASIL *accepts her white flag. They've reached an armistice.*

BASIL: Roger, pass those pages.

> ROGER *waves his arm in the direction of the newspaper and makes pissweak baby noises. He's not getting up for* BASIL.

There's something I need to know.

> *Still no genuine attempt from* ROGER …

> BASIL *retrieves the newspaper, slapping his friend on the way past.*

When I first took an interest in Delia, I dug around a bit.
ROGER: [*to* MARIE] He opened a newspaper for her. A manual newspaper. It was awesome.
BASIL: Hey, you asked me to look at the wider world, didn't you? I couldn't see the obvious then, but—
ROGER: You still can't see the obvious. You have the intellectual capacity of a PEZ dispenser.

All investment burned; ROGER *lies flat. He's tapping out.*

BASIL *concentrates on* MARIE.

BASIL: This was taken a few years ago. Delia and her friends. It's the anniversary of their protest, when they chained themselves up to prank some loggers, and—

MARIE: And you want to know why your father was there.

Instant silence. Heavy. Deafening.

BASIL: [*shocked*] You didn't even glance at the page.

ROGER *sits up.*

So, it wasn't all random …

The two men exchange troubled expressions.

Delia finding me. The funeral. The dance.

BASIL *drops the paper on* ROGER.

ROGER: [*studying the page*] We were so focussed on her, we never even considered—

BASIL: *I'm sick of the lies.* [*To* MARIE] You've been hovering around this situation like a …

ROGER: Sparrowhawk?

BASIL: A vulture, picking over the shreds of some old story, some old resentment. I don't need you to manipulate my decisions, I need you to be direct. That's supposed to be what you're good at, isn't it?

MARIE: …

BASIL: For once, trust me enough to share your plans with me.

She'd like to, but … instead, MARIE *fobs him off.*

MARIE: [*airily*] Where did that explosion come from?

BASIL: Deep in my soul, where it has been festering for years. Don't expect me to swallow it back down.

Calm, but resolute, he draws closer to her.

You knew who she was. When you came here and pretended to be piecing it together, you *knew*.

ROGER *rises to stand by* BASIL'*s side.*

You knew because *he* knew.

ROGER: Who is she?

Pause.

MARIE: She's one of his.

> *Something escapes* MARIE.
>
> *Something like a chuckle, something like a sob.*

Your father was so kind. Effortlessly kind.

> *She can't bring herself to look at her son.*

He'd weave his words, hand out his dreams … and they were his.

ROGER: Lovers?

MARIE: Never.

BASIL: Disciples.

> *Another pause. The nod is subtle. Pained.*

MARIE: He was always faithful to me … But, that was nothing compared to how faithful they were to him.

> *At last, she turns to confront* BASIL.

I never doubted his view of the world. If we don't condemn cruelty, then what is the point of us? Plants need that oxygen, don't they, Roger?

ROGER: Well, they require a certain amount to—

BASIL: If you and Dad were so alike, so sure, what / happened?

MARIE: *You* happened.

> *Beat.*

We'd been marked for years. Profiled. *Listed.* You didn't have to carry that stain.

BASIL: I feel like you'll never take me seriously.

MARIE: [*a small smile*] It's possible, but dubious.

> *She admires the horizon.*

So, we did what all broken activists do. We retreated to a cosseted city and pretended we had no idea how much suffering went into every aspect of who and what we had become. My duck-down quilt, my leather bag …

> *Her fingers rise to touch her mouth.*

The scream painted on my lips.

> BASIL *takes a further step closer to her. She rounds on him.*

And now you're looking down your nose at the very people who allow us to play make-believe ... the people who plunge their hands in blood so that we / don't have to.

BASIL: I have to *do* something. I won't be apathetic.

MARIE: And I adore you for that.

Mother and son see each other clearly.

You've found yourself.

BASIL: It's all broken. The whole world.

MARIE: [*nodding*] Only none of us know how to fix it.

For the first time, they may hug ... without it being stilted, or accomplished with alcohol.

BASIL: [*smirking*] Hippie parents. I reckon I should've seen that coming.

MARIE: ...?

BASIL: My name is Basil Pepper.

MARIE *breaks into a smile.*

MARIE: It seemed profound at the time.

She cups his chin.

But, learn from us. Know that an idea can rot your insides.

ROGER: It might be too late.

MARIE: And if you commit yourself to that idea, if you follow it wherever it leads you ...

ROGER: We should hide him, Marie.

MARIE: I warned your father to be mindful. Prophets breed fanatics.

BASIL: Delia is *not* a fanatic.

ROGER: Have I evaporated again?

BASIL: Somewhere. Somehow. Something has to *matter*.

MARIE: There are limits, Basil. An idea can grind you, regardless of how worthy it may be.

BASIL *shakes his mother away.*

BASIL: You and Dad were wrong to give up. We'll take it further than you ever did. *True radicals.* The bowling ladies won't like *that* will they, Mum?

Pause.

MARIE: My beautiful boy, if I could write a happy ending for you, I would ... But this wound will keep tearing ...

ROGER: *Marie!*

BASIL: I won't go back to sleep.

ROGER: *Basil!*

MARIE: She may be brilliant, but that mind will *never* be satisfied.

ROGER: *Both of you listen!*

> *They finally acknowledge* ROGER ...

> *He checks his pulse.*

Right. Lovely. Still here.

> *They open their mouths.*

No! Quiet time! Basil needs to get away from this building. The maintenance man knows I was handcuffed.

MARIE: Who?

ROGER: The fellow in the hard hat and the inappropriate shorts. You saw him. [*Light bulb*] *Spigot!*

MARIE: Spigot?

ROGER: Bubba Spigot.

BASIL: The guy's name is Bubba Spigot?

ROGER: It's a professional name, like Captain Birdseye or Joe Camel.

BASIL: [*the penny clattering*] Or Artemis Vermouth.

ROGER: You of all people should understand, Barry. Still, he might come back with help and you don't want to be here when ... Barry? Basil dear?

> BASIL *has returned to his backpack.*

BASIL: Take my mother home.

MARIE: Sod that, I'm staying right—

> *She freezes.*

> *Her son has a pistol in his hand.*

Think carefully.

ROGER: He's clearly not doing that.

> *He's too busy trembling.*

> *And from the fire escape—from everywhere—come the* SNOOPS.
> BASIL *steadies himself.*

MARIE: Darling, take a shot and your life is over. Be smarter than that. Be patient.

NORMAN: Mother knows best.
ROGER: [*frowning*] Spigot …?
BASIL: [*glaring*] Vermouth.

> *They're both wrong.*

> *A gap in the* SNOOPS *opens up, and* NORMAN *fills it. He tips his hat.*

NORMAN: Special Officer Norman Gould.
ROGER: Christ, I let you near my sink.
NORMAN: We just want to ask you some questions, Mr Pepper.
ROGER: I hope you're handier with a wrench than you are with a bottle.

> BASIL *raises his weapon.*

> *Don't be nuts, Barry!*

BASIL: [*controlled*] Get out of my way, Roger.

> *The* SNOOPS *drop their gloves to their belts.* NORMAN *shakes his head.*

MARIE: They hardly have anything on you. Don't give them this.

> BASIL *clicks the safety off.*

BASIL: [*a warning*] Roger.
ROGER: [*freaking out*] Barry!

> *It's difficult to know what happens first …* BASIL *tries to sidestep* ROGER … ROGER *tries to tackle* BASIL.

> *Neither quite manages it. A shot rings out.*

BASIL: *Mum!*

> MARIE *grabs her arm, and falls down with a grunt.*

> BASIL *hurries over to her, while* ROGER *sways in shock … and an amused* NORMAN *calmly retrieves the pistol, covering it with a handkerchief, despite his gloves.*

> *Clearly,* MARIE *is more surprised than hurt. And more pissed off than surprised.*

MARIE: Oh, Basil …

> *She glares at her gormless child.*

> This is so *you.*

> *Blackout.*

SCENE EIGHT

Under the bare bulb.

BASIL *stares at the tape recorder. Long pause.*

BASIL: And now you're up to speed.

> NORMAN *gives him an indulgent smile.*

You can't keep me here forever.

NORMAN: Only until you cooperate.

> *He sits opposite* BASIL.

BASIL: So, who is Norman Gould? A faceless man? One of those suits who carries out the bidding of tin pot dictators?

NORMAN: Show some respect.

BASIL: Earn it.

> *Beat.*

I can imagine your résumé. Thatcherite. Brexiteer. Trumpkin.

NORMAN: Manners.

BASIL: Why?

NORMAN: He's the president.

BASIL: [*with a shrug*] Eh, the jury's still out.

NORMAN: …

BASIL: Hey, man, tell it to the Allies. They didn't fight fascism in the forties to see it redecorating the White House now.

NORMAN: The election was / final.

BASIL: Hitler won an election too. That doesn't make it a good day.

> NORMAN *opens a manila folder.*

NORMAN: You lean to the left, then?

BASIL: I'm left-wing, but if anyone calls me a communist … I'll call them an idiot.

NORMAN: [*amused*] A progressive?

BASIL: Sure.

NORMAN: With tree spikes?

> *A tense beat.*

BASIL: You don't get to threaten half the population and not suffer a backlash. The left has been too sweet for too long. Politeness and complacency won't move mountains.

NORMAN: I see. The liberal intelligentsia gets to throw a hissy fit whenever things don't go their way?

BASIL: Well, it's better than goose-stepping, Norm.

> BASIL's *palms hit the table.*

NORMAN: How could anyone compare Trump to / Hitler?

BASIL: [*pushing hard*] It's an accurate historical parallel. [*Off his stare*] Sorry, did those big words frighten you?

NORMAN: We're not in—

BASIL: America blows its nose and we sneeze.

> *Beat.*

> NORMAN *actually laughs.*

NORMAN: Now, that was *almost* convincing. Your friend certainly taught you the playbook of middle-class clichés. Bravo, Mr Pepper.

BASIL: …

NORMAN: You're dancing with me. I don't make time for people who waste it.

> *He gestures and* SNOOPS *enter, peeling out from the shadows.*

You're not red, Mr Pepper.

BASIL: …

NORMAN: You're green.

> *The* SNOOPS *place* BASIL's *gun on the table.*

BASIL: It's licensed.

NORMAN: That works for Bond, but not for you. [*Smiling*] Let's start again. Honestly.

> *He waves the* SNOOPS *away.*

This isn't about the bourgeoisie versus the proletariat, or making any nation great. You don't care about the cuckoos in the White House. You don't care about class or cloth, or creed. This is something much more primal. Something at the centre of your identity.

> *Pause.*

[*Quietly*] I know you, Mr Pepper. I make my living from those who love too much.

BASIL: …

NORMAN: Who am I, you ask? My portfolio is very specific. Ecoterrorism: the new wave of anarchy. Rabble-rousers, like your Delia.

BASIL: She's not my—

NORMAN: Virtue signallers who fail to confront life's grim by-line …

> BASIL *waits.*

> NORMAN *knits his fingers.*

Nature is cruel.

> *Pause.*

> BASIL *leans back in his chair.*

BASIL: Nature gives you a head start.

NORMAN: …

BASIL: Tell me, what's so natural about being born in a cage, or getting ripped away from your mother?

NORMAN: This isn't a / debate.

BASIL: Can you appreciate how fucking weird that is? Being torn from your mother's breast so that she can give milk to *an entirely different species.* That's not 'nature'. That's some kind of fetish.

> *He stands.*

Everything you're defending is warped.

NORMAN: And legal.

> *Beat.*

And accepted.

BASIL: …

NORMAN: You've become an extremist, Mr Pepper.

> BASIL *looks down at* NORMAN *with sincere astonishment.*

BASIL: Open your eyes.

NORMAN: Your mother has argued on your behalf. I will give you precisely one opportunity to escape prosecution. [*Smirking*] Help me get Delia on the record.

BASIL: There's *nothing* you can pin on her. I'm all you've got … and I'm not great.

NORMAN: People like her are eroding our national values.

BASIL: Sure, let's blame the bleeding hearts.

NORMAN: Let's.

BASIL: [*bursting*] When the air blisters with our poison, when we're all choking on the stink of our negligence and greed … and the last living thing that isn't one of us is flattened or gutted, or served with a side of fries … let's blame the *fucking hippies*, Norm. That makes sense.

NORMAN: I can slap your wrist. Or cuff it.

Beat.

BASIL: [*defiantly*] You're wrong about her.

MARIE: When someone tells you who they are, believe them.

MARIE *has entered.*

She won't stop at tree spikes.

BASIL: How do you know?

MARIE: Because *I* didn't.

BASIL *looks down at her sling. He has no words. No fight. He drops back into his chair to bury his head.*

She'll think bigger than the farms, bigger than billboards or speeches, or appeals to people's better nature. She knows there's no such thing.

NORMAN: When we bugged the flat, she spoke of corporations. She may target the—

BASIL: Dead cow industry.

The walls close in.

That's her interest.

He feels their eyes on him. Wilts under the weight of their expectation.

MARIE: [*to* NORMAN] He can get her to talk.

NORMAN: [*nodding*] Freedom is conditional. [*A thin smile*] I'll release you back into the wild, but you're branded now. When this is over, if I were you, I'd sniff out another mate.

BASIL *nods his acquiescence.*

You've lost her, regardless. She has no room for grey. No patience for the uncertain.

NORMAN *rises. He has never looked taller.*

The day is coming when the world will be cleft between 'them' and 'us'. Find your certainty before that day sneaks up on you. Before the line is drawn, and the ink is dry.

MARIE: My son is not a radical.

BASIL: I … Don't make me …

> *Something human crosses* NORMAN*'s eyes.*

> *Something close to sympathy.*

NORMAN: You wear your heart on your sleeve, Mr Pepper. Anyone can reach out and take it.

> *The bulb flickers, and fades.*

SCENE NINE

The roof.

BASIL *finds* ROGER *sprawled out on his deckchair. Stars gleam over their heads, peeking through smog.*

ROGER: How are you?

BASIL: I'm a flat, emotionless line … You?

ROGER: Well-oiled.

> *He stands and passes* BASIL *a glass of brandy. He's trying to be light.*

There's no dodging this bullet, my friend. In some ways you've been lucky.

BASIL: …

ROGER: Fine, not lucky per se, but they'll let you go if—

BASIL: *If I entrap her.*

> *He turns away to swallow his shame.*

> *He laughs sourly.*

I hate that I've become a hurtful thing in her life. We were supposed to be happy. [*Looking down at the streets*] We were supposed to be invincible.

> *He hands his glass to* ROGER.

I'm moving out.

ROGER: Piffle, dear boy … this is a blip. I can still / guide you.

BASIL: You're shallow, Roger.

Nobody is laughing now.

Do you know what I was thinking about in that tiny room, while Norman was grilling me ...? I was thinking, 'This is what Benjamin felt like'.

ROGER: Who's Benjamin?

BASIL: The last Tasmanian tiger.

ROGER: Oh, grow / up.

BASIL: It's stupid, it's sentimental ... *but I can't get him out of my fucking head!*

ROGER *is shocked by the intensity of* BASIL's *conviction.*

BASIL *laughs again, but it's a desperate laugh.*

I see the world through her eyes now. I see pigs on spits, and I remember that pigs are smarter than dogs. I see fur coats and imagine the horror of being born to be *skinned*. I see ... I dunno, fat morons eating hamburgers ... and I want to *smash their dumb, smug faces!*

He drives his fist into his palm.

And I'm not wrong. On a basic, human level I'm *not wrong*. [*Tapping his head*] But I *am* wrong, because you can't live in this world with all of those screams echoing in here.

ROGER: She has indoctrinated / you, Basil.

BASIL: And you, y' champagne lefty ... Moscato Lord, dribbling bullshit down your chin ... what do *you* stand for? If I asked you, right now, to change your lifestyle ... to shift one tiny atom of your routine, you'd call me—

ROGER: A friend. Nothing else.

BASIL: Let's start with the car. Six-seater. Even *your* arse isn't / that big.

ROGER: [*haughtily*] I don't like what she's turned you into.

BASIL: You're a hypocrite, mate. You're boring.

ROGER: Shall I cuff myself again?

BASIL: You *love* to shake your finger when others don't measure up, but you've never done *anything* constructive yourself. This world is crying out and I want to answer. That's who I am. *That's* what I care about.

ROGER: [*stung*] What about what *I* care about?

BASIL: [*closing in*] You *don't* care. So, you rot. Alone.

ROGER *slumps back down into his deckchair. He has never looked so gutted, so fearful ... or so tiny.*

ROGER: I have done something constructive.

Even he isn't sure if he's laughing, or crying ...

You may think me a buffoon, but I knew this building was under surveillance. I said the word: Sparrowhawk.

BASIL: Sparrowhawk?

ROGER: He told me to use it if I was in danger. I always suspected we were dealing with Artemis / Vermouth.

BASIL: [*correcting him*] Norman Gould.

ROGER: I always suspected we were dealing with Norman—

BASIL: You weren't in any danger. [*Darkly*] Not then.

The threat is very real.

ROGER: Is this some kind of God complex? Thinking you can change the world …

BASIL: *I can change me!*

ROGER *flinches.*

[*Calmer*] I can change me. That matters.

BASIL*'s temper cools, but only because* ROGER *is so submissive.* ROGER *pours himself a second—or maybe it's his fifth—drink.*

Pause.

ROGER: So, you're choosing the anarchist over your friend?

BASIL: Over everyone.

ROGER: Because she thrills you? Or because being close to her lets you imagine that you have her courage?

This hits home. BASIL *flinches. He gives* ROGER *some ground.*

Don't tell me it's love, Basil.

BASIL: She makes me real.

ROGER: She makes you crazy. A few weeks ago, you were *nothing* … now you're worse. You're a muppet.

He snorts.

Infatuation. Naïveté. The Manic Pixie Dream Girl and her obsequious golem.

BASIL: Shut your—

ROGER: *The banality stings.*

BASIL: I changed for you, so I can change for her.

ROGER: [*jeering*] It was *always* for her. That's why it won't last.

BASIL: Why can't / you let me go?

ROGER: [*shredding*] You can't be what she needs you to be. Nobody can.

BASIL: …

ROGER: Humans aren't built that way, alright? We're not brave, we're not selfless. When we see something wrong, we turn away, we keep driving, we wait for some … mythical grown-up to take care of it. We're weak.

> BASIL *takes this in.*

We're mercenary.

> *He rallies …*

BASIL: For me then. I'll change for me.

> *But it's hollow.* ROGER *tastes blood.*

ROGER: Would you look at that? [*Caustically*] Pinocchio thinks his heart is beating.

> BASIL *turns his back and exits, leaving* ROGER *alone with the stars.*

It's you or her, Basil.

> *This is the last they'll say to each other. Silence.*
>
> *Regret.*
>
> *And then … thunder.*

SCENE TEN

Red lights.

'The World We Made' by Ruelle heralds the end of days. The final gambit.

Downstage left, BASIL *finds himself strapping a microphone to his body once again. This time the equipment is much more sophisticated … frighteningly subtle.*

Downstage right, DELIA *strides out in her corporate pinstripes, swiping an ID card and smiling at someone unseen.*

BASIL *zips up his chameleon costume.*

DELIA *places her briefcase on the floor.*

BASIL *takes a deep breath. Lets it out. His head is down.*

DELIA *opens the case. Shuts it again. Her hackles are up. And now, the shadows are here ...*

SNOOPS *close in and block the exits. We're all trapped now.*

Sensing rather than seeing them, BASIL *and* DELIA *come together, centre stage. The music erupts.*

Upstage left, ROGER *empties bottles. Sobering up, planning for tomorrow.*

Upstage right, MARIE *paces. Hoping her son will make the right decision, but not knowing what that is.*

The SNOOPS *turn, synchronously, and stand at attention—a repeated meme of trilbies, trench coats and silent menace.*

They part.

Someone else is here ...

A silhouette. Slim. Graceful. Serpentine. NORMAN *waits. He is confident. Mistakenly so.*

When the music dies, the storm is reborn. BASIL *and* DELIA *face each other.*

BASIL: You lied to me.

DELIA: Did I?

BASIL: My father. You knew him.

DELIA: I did.

BASIL: So, what am I to you? The heir apparent?

DELIA: You know that's—

BASIL: Do you even *see* me?

     DELIA *crosses to him. She doesn't blink.*

DELIA: Every day. Every second. Of course I see you.

     BASIL *rolls his eyes.*

Hey, I was searching for *you.* Howard was kind, but he wasn't brave.

     They regard each other with new insecurity.

He wasn't selfless and humble, and funny, and / beautiful.

BASIL: Where are the others, Delia? Why were you left so alone?

DELIA: …

BASIL: Mum said there was a cult. A 'movement' that Dad inspired. What happened to—?

DELIA: *What do you think happened?!*

BASIL: …

DELIA: Yes, I was alone. [*Losing all confidence*] Am I still alone?

Beat.

It was you who never really saw me. I was honest. I showed you my fangs.

BASIL: I'd hoped you'd settle down, but you're so militant, and to / confront that—

DELIA: To confront that, you'd have to acknowledge the person here …

She passes her hand over her face.

… instead of the person here.

She touches his heart.

BASIL *is instantly remorseful. The storm simmers.*

BASIL: I can't go back now. That was the point, wasn't it? Mum tried to protect me, but …

He trails off. DELIA *softens.*

DELIA: But she didn't have that right. I showed you behind the curtain.

BASIL: To punish me?

BASIL *takes a step back.*

DELIA: To rescue you.

He isn't buying it.

BASIL: Mum and Dad betrayed you when they had me. They sold you out. You and all the friends you've lost.

DELIA: I don't blame—

BASIL: You do. [*Kindly*] That's why you opened my eyes, Delia. I'm grateful that you did. But I'll hurt … I'll scream, for the rest of my life. That's your revenge.

He reaches into his plush costume and shows off his voice recorder.

This is mine.

He presses a button.

NORMAN: [*voice only*] *Freedom is conditional.*
DELIA: That'll play well to the press gallery.
NORMAN: [*voice only*] *The world will be cleft between 'them' and 'us'.*

> DELIA *cracks a smile.*

BASIL: Six years of panto.
DELIA: My little chameleon.

> *She takes the recording.*

BASIL: I've got backups. [*Sincerely*] He can't follow you anymore, Delia.
DELIA: There will always be another one. Another three. A dozen.

> *The recording slips into* DELIA*'s jacket.*

Maybe humans are supposed to lose everything.

> *She returns to her cases.*

Maybe we're too shallow to claw our way out of this mess.

> BASIL *takes this in.*

BASIL: [*rallying*] There's a chance you can help the others. Expose Norman, demonstrate that they were unjustly targeted, and … you won't be alone anymore.

> *He watches her …*

> *The bravest, fiercest person he's ever met.*

I see you now. Roger called you a pixie … But, you're ferocious … certain …
DELIA: *He's* a pixie.
BASIL: [*with a sad smile*] You're an orc.

> *His smile fades.*

I can't chase you anymore.

> DELIA *nods, even as her smile fades too.*

Because I'm average.
DELIA: …
BASIL: Because you're a tiger, and I'm not.

> *He looks down at his costume.*

I'm built to blend in with my environment.

> *Long pause.*

DELIA *closes her eyes. Puffs out her disenchantment. Laughs at him.*

DELIA: Oh, Basil. Is this your plan? You … let me go? I waltz into the sunset to have quinoa with Greta Thunberg?

BASIL: You have Norman's words in your pocket. Use them to drum up—

DELIA: I can't beg people to change. I can't yell. I can't reason. *I can't wait.*

BASIL: Delia, these people will hunt you.

DELIA: You're too nice, do you know that? Too patient. Tolerant. Sitting on the fence won't save the world.

BASIL: Please—

DELIA: *You don't get to be my martyr, Basil.*

And she's angry now.

Still laughing, still mocking him … but fucking angry.

All this time sharing my bed, and you never even checked the address. You never wondered … 'Why this house?', 'Did she break in here for a reason?' 'What's so special about this particular family, holidaying abroad, with their Dalmatians and their sexy BMW?' [*Grinning*] Come on, Basil. Here, boy. Let me teach you a new trick.

She kneels before her briefcase.

BASIL: The house? I—I just thought it was … random.

DELIA: I get it. Your father was fixated on the beginning too. The factory farms. That's where all the blood is. All the death. But this is the end of the chain. This is where they manage their message, and reap their rewards.

BASIL *kneels beside her.*

The government has its hand in the trough. That's not being cute, that's a statement of fact. A lot of senators are farmers. They are literally the landed gentry.

The lid flips up.

We can't expect our friend Norman to serve the people. If he did, he'd be on my side. The people are going to face drought, famine, riots, storms that will swallow nations and social decay that will rot

their faith and eat their laws. The end of apathy. The end of five billion lazy lives.

BASIL: Five billion?

DELIA: [*nodding*] When you exclude the wretchedly poor and the greedy
as fuck.

> *She shifts the case away from* BASIL, *as he gets too curious. It's a
> trick case ... A second compartment opens.*

Norman serves vested interests. Embedded ideas. But all the conviction in the universe won't change reality. He's going to lose, Basil.
[*Winking*] Even without a goddess standing in his way.

BASIL: Is that really how you see yourself?

DELIA: The goddess Delia. Huntress. Butcher. [*With a shrug*] It's not
very me, is it? But she was also the protector of wild animals. She
enforced the balance between predator and prey.

> *There is a rush of cold air from the case, a burst of refrigerator
> steam.*

And she was a dancer too. She led the Muses and the Graces. But, you
know what else she did, Basil? When she had to? She brought disease,
pestilence ... the sudden death of six children, so that one may thrive.

> BASIL *'s world is melting. He backs away from the case.*

So ... what kind of job gets you Dalmatians, a BMW, that shower we
both enjoyed, and oodles of frequent flyer points? I bet it's something
really, *really* risky.

BASIL: [*overcome*] You can't hurt / people.

DELIA: People won't change. It's easy to care about a cause when it
doesn't affect you ... But, when it does, profit drives behaviour.
Profit and convenience.

BASIL: And terror?

DELIA: *We make terror.* Swine flu is what happens when you lock thousands of pigs with their own filth. Mad cow is the quirky consequence
of feeding animal remains to animals that don't eat remains.

> *The case hisses.*

You said it yourself. E. coli. Salmonella. That makes them pause.
What d'you think it'll take to make them stop?

BASIL: Nobody has that right.

DELIA: Cruelty is a choice. Apathy is a choice.

> *Her convictions firm,* DELIA *slams the case shut ... but not before slipping something into her pocket.*

When a species grows too fast, too hungry, we murder them. Isn't that playing God?

> BASIL *opens his mouth to refute her ... discovers he can't.*

BASIL: I honestly don't know.

DELIA: We released the calicivirus without batting an eye, even as it turned little bunny eyes to mush. That was for the farms too, wasn't it? So we could go on eating, spreading ...

BASIL: Choking.

> *He approaches her.*

But, Delia, you're better than that. You're better than revenge.

DELIA: Anthrax would be revenge. Melioidosis. Q fever. The problem is they target ... [*Correcting herself*] They *kill*, indiscriminately.

> *She traces her finger around the case. With her free hand, she invites* BASIL *to look closer.*

Revenge is facile. Revenge is small. I want change.

BASIL: [*reading*] Limos. [*Looking up*] It isn't the name of the couple who live here ...

DELIA: It's the name of their laboratory. The name of their mistake. Their crisis. [*A grin*] Their gift.

> BASIL *treats the case like it's a toxic thing. He backs away, visibly shaken.*

Like most of the terrors that spread in this world, it was a solution to a problem we caused. It was supposed to target infected herds, to stop mad cow, but in the lab it decided to do a Delia and misbehave.

BASIL: [*urgently*] You don't *have* to / misbehave.

DELIA: The virus is airborne. Technically, it's a retrovirus, a little work-shop of creative enzymes. It clings to a host, invades their cells and changes them, permanently.

BASIL: Changes them?

DELIA: How many cows are out there? Conservatively, around one and a half billion ... And they only have to breathe it to carry it. Once

it finds them, it inserts its genome and replicates. No, this isn't sci-
fi, it's a natural reservoir of disease. The way mosquitoes spread
malaria. I'm changing the game, Basil. [*Smiling coldly*] I'm turning
victims into hunters.

BASIL: How it will it change them?

DELA: In an uncontrolled environment, it'll spread faster than influenza,
faster than measles … and much, *much* faster than Norman Gould.

BASIL: *What happens if you let it out?*

DELIA: The goddess takes wing. She finds a stall, a cage, a country. She
infects. She multiples. She flies again.

BASIL: And can we stop—?

DELIA: *Have we stopped the common cold?*

> *Lightning.*

BASIL: You're letting Death out of a bottle.

DELIA: Death is here. I'm giving Her clarity.

BASIL: It's mad.

DELIA: It's hope.

> *She can see that he's afraid …*

> *Beat.*

> *She raises her hands. Tempers herself.*

There's beauty in this, Basil. The virus can't spread between human
beings, not without invading an animal host and rewriting them from
the inside. To catch it, a person would have to—

BASIL: Eat them.

> *He stares. Pennies clatter in his mind's eye.*

Eat an infected animal.

> DELIA *grins. She knows she has captured his imagination.*

DELIA: It wouldn't be the first time this has ever happened, babe. Zoonotic
pathogens have biblical pedigree. There were only nine plagues of
Egypt, not ten. The fifth plague struck the cattle … the sixth infected
the humans. [*Reaching out*] But not *all* the humans. Just the ones who
didn't stop to think.

> *She clasps his hands. Squeezes them tight.*

Cruelty. Apathy. They cost.

BASIL: …

DELIA: Either the world boils and we all die, or we turn the choice into something they can understand. It's *fair*, Basil.

> *The storm roars.*

You see me now, don't you?

BASIL: They're / watching.

DELIA: *I want them to watch me.*

MARIE: Delia …

> *Lightning.*

> MARIE *is suddenly there. And* DELIA *is holding a vial.*

Let him go.

DELIA: Oh look, a baby boomer spitting the dummy.

MARIE: He's innocent.

DELIA: All animals are innocent, even—

MARIE: 'Even when they bite.' I remember. People, on the other hand, have evolved to hold grudges.

DELIA: That they have, Marie. [*Stone cold*] You left me behind.

MARIE: We made a choice, for our child. I stand by that choice. [*Cautiously*] Will you stand by yours, Delia?

DELIA: …

MARIE: See, I don't think you will. For the same exact reason. He's a pinhead, but he's very hard not to love.

> DELIA *looks back at* BASIL. *She is wrestling with herself …* *Fighting not to cry, or to relent …*

DELIA: I wasn't supposed to like you this much.

MARIE: I'd take a bullet for my boy. I did. Because he is such a fu—

BASIL: Alright, Mum. [*To* DELIA] You don't have to do this.

DELIA: It's who I am.

BASIL: You don't have to do this alone.

MARIE: Basil?

BASIL: [*hardening*] When someone tells you who they are, believe them.

DELIA: We break this vial, we change the world.

> BASIL *kisses her. She holds onto him.*

BASIL: Roger was finally right. It's me or you.

He steps back. The vial is in his hand. Even DELIA *is shocked.*

Their eyes were on the tiger, but they should've been looking at the lizard.

DELIA: Are you certain?

BASIL: Completely. I love everything you are. [*With a big grin*] Hey, Mum … Watch this!

He slams the vial down.

MARIE *is speechless, but not as appalled as she might have been. The flicker of a smile.*

Police lights. Sirens. Music.

Go. [*To* MARIE] You have to get her away from here. *Hide her!*

MARIE *nods and takes* DELIA *by the hand.*

DELIA *resists.*

But the stage is chaotic. SNOOPS *are swarming.*

It looks like DELIA *won't move, but* BASIL *urges her on. Finally,* DELIA *leans in …*

And whispers in his ear.

BASIL *watches, shattered, as she runs out of his world.*

The SNOOPS *pass. Giving chase. The sirens fade with their footsteps.* BASIL *is left in silence.*

He turns and flicks on the projector. Benjamin paces his cage.

Exhausted now, BASIL *sinks to the floor. He watches until the music ends, and the night is still.*

A shadow stretches across the screen …

NORMAN: What a hopeless image.

Beat.

BASIL: Not with her out there.

NORMAN *stands over* BASIL. *He is his eternal self—the suited shadow—vigilant and untiring.*

NORMAN: I took your advice. Gave her a head start.

BASIL *smiles.*

BASIL: Every instinct is telling me to give chase, to run with her in the rain forever …

He stares up at NORMAN.

But this isn't a fairytale.

NORMAN: No. [*Stepping back*] Regrettably not.

The two men watch each other.

BASIL: There's nothing you can do now. The genie's loose, Norm. [*Standing*] And you've been brought into the light. I don't want you coming near me, or my family, ever again.

NORMAN *nods. It's curt, but respectful.*

BASIL *turns to leave.*

NORMAN: Will this be a better world?

BASIL: It'll be a world.

NORMAN: Tell me what she whispered to you. That night you danced together.

BASIL: You don't get to see everything.

He touches his own heart.

You don't get to look in here.

Shadows converge …

SNOOPS, *returning to support their chief.* NORMAN *raises a hand, keeping his wolves at bay.*

NORMAN: We'll be watching you, Mr Pepper.

BASIL: You still don't get it, Norm.

He offers his open palms.

We'll be watching you too.

With that, BASIL *leaves it all behind.*

His dignity affronted, NORMAN *takes a second to tip his hat and straighten his collar.*

Then his eyes return to the flickering image.

He removes a glove.

And reaches out.

THE END

S A P T

SOUTH
AUSTRALIAN
PLAYWRIGHTS
THEATRE

presents

WATCHLIST

Playwright
Alex Vickery-Howe

Director
Lisa Harper Campbell

Producer
Lucy Combe

Lighting Designer
Stephen Dean

Sound Designer
Sascha Budimski

Stage Manager
Clare Miyuki Guerin

Set Construction
David Adams

Basil – **Gianluca Noble**

Marie – **Katie O'Reilly**

Delia – **Katherine Sortini**

Roger – **Eddie Morrison**

Norman – **Matt Hawkins**

WRITER'S NOTE

I've been questioned by the police four times.

Not for doing anything, or even for saying anything. Just for walking.

I went through a beardy stage in my late 20s and wore a duffle coat. That was enough to be profiled. I'll admit one time I was loitering outside Kirribilli—that probably looked a little suss—but for the most part I was just going about my day. One police officer had Bowie's 'Ashes to Ashes' for his ringtone and blushed mid-grilling. Another refused to believe me when I said I was waiting for a pizza to cook ... he demanded to know which franchise was making the pizza and what the topping was (answer: Domino's, Vegorama, thin crust. I have the napkin to prove it, your honour.)

This was the first spark that led to *Watchlist*.

Later, as I rounded the corner from my 20s to my 30s, there was a popular Coalition booklet that made me scratch my skanky beard. It was the culmination of a paranoia that had begun, justifiably enough, in the context of genuine security threats, but spiraled into the surreal.

The booklet—hilarious, if only it were a Shaun Micallef sketch—asked parents to watch out for the tell-tale signs that their son or daughter was being radicalised. Signs like the 'alternative music scene', 'student politics', 'overseas events', and failing to 'entirely trust the government or police' because 'it takes a long time to change some habits of thinking'.

Thought Police aside, you had to wonder if then-Justice Minister Michael Keenan had ever been a teenager when he and his staff listed 'anxiety' and 'depression' as key indicators of radicalisation. At the time, #freeKaren, #IamKaren and #JeSuisKaren trended, as the (presumably) fictional case study of Karen—a young woman who 'attended an environmental protest with some of her friends' and dared to find it 'exhilarating'—struck balanced humans around the country as a pretty ridiculous example of someone supposedly going off the rails.

Luckily for the 1.5 humans (Michael is the .5) gnashing their teeth for Karen, she was soon assimilated back into society when she chose to embrace a 'more moderate eco-philosophy'; hey, we can't possibly have people genuinely caring about the environment and willing to do something about it. That's radical.

For me, it was funny, then baffling, and then a bit worrisome. How did the environmental movement strike these people as more dangerous than white supremacy, religious extremism, or ... anything that had actually cost human lives? And then my own paranoia kicked in.

Should I stop recycling? Will the government see my compost bucket as a hate sign? Is David Attenborough an 'extremist' now?

The booklet was the second spark. Brandis was the third.

When Attorney General George Brandis—don't y'all miss him?—became interested in our metadata, despite the storage nightmare this posed for ISPs (a classic old man's grasp of new technology), I realised that the once reliable line between surreal and mainstream was starting to splinter, if not flake away. More insidiously, Old George dipped into his personal Dark Web, like Gargamel, and conjured 'counterterrorism' laws that would allow ASIO agents to get handsy, or punish whistleblowers … paving the way for the public vilification of journalists; our latest international sport.

But, come on, we had a democracy to protect … or something like a democracy … I mean, we wouldn't be eroding *all* of our principles, just the inconvenient ones. What's a little light torture if it saves lives? We're only selling a tiny slice of our soul.

I collected these sparks and kept them warm. And then came the fire. Naomi Wolf's book *The End of America: Letter of Warning to a Young Patriot* (2007), and documentary (2008), set the sparks ablaze. Wolf outlines the ten steps of a 'closing society':

1. Invoke a terrifying internal and external enemy.

2. Create secret prisons where torture takes place.

3. Develop a thug caste or paramilitary force not answerable to citizens.

4. Set up an internal surveillance system.

5. Infiltrate and harass citizens' groups.

6. Engage in arbitrary detention and release.

7. Target key individuals.

8. Control the press.

9. Cast criticism as espionage and dissent as treason.

10. Subvert the rule of law.

I owe my title to Wolf. She asserts that everyday citizens are being placed on a 'watchlist' for criticising the American government. This includes grass roots activists, artists and academics. People who are considered dangerous for their words alone.

Fast forward to 2019 and the Trump administration horror show is even checking tourists' social media history before they are granted entry to the United States. I'm screwed. Goodbye Comic-Con.

Like Wolf, I find it increasingly astounding how many civil liberties are being violated in the name of 'freedom'. Bowie's 'This Is Not America' is the song for our ringtones now; a haunting epitaph to the second decade of the 21st century.

In Australia, as Keenan's booklet demonstrates, the thought of the innocent and the hapless ending up on the watchlist is not so far-fetched. It all comes down to security versus liberty: how much do we increase one at the expense of the other?

This is the premise of *Watchlist*, wherein innocent and hapless Basil Pepper finds his way onto the government's radar, because he tries to impress a left-leaning love interest.

It's comedic. It's also scary.

When devising a world around Basil, I invented an ensemble of clashing personalities. Two of them, I'm not too ashamed to admit, represent two conflicting sides of my own character.

I believe, very passionately, in everything Delia stands for: tougher animal rights legislation, in particular stronger penalties for animal cruelty; responsibility for the pain our choices cause; a fearless attitude ... and a healthy disregard for social graces in the face of smug cruelty.

I'm a little bit in love with her.

As I researched the environmental consequences of factory farming and, unfortunately, farming in general, I found myself drawn more into Delia's reasoning. I asked myself, what is the line between activism and terrorism? When does passion become too extreme? And what is 'sane' at this critical moment in history? It is not only ethically reprehensible—although humans shy away from that argument—but it is incredibly and demonstrably stupid to pretend that we can keep abusing our planet, and every living creature upon it, without consequence. Sanity, therefore, demands action.

Delia is right about that. Delia I understand.

But I'm scared of turning into Roger ... What a wet tit is Roger. Pretentious. Well-meaning. Pissweak.

Roger represents the other half of my thinking, the flippant and shallow half, who is concerned more with pointing out what's wrong than with doing what's right. Roger, nevertheless, can function in our society; Delia is outside it, beyond it.

I've left Basil and the audience trapped between these two irreconcilable perspectives. The walker and the talker. The tiger and the sloth.

In the end, the guts of the play is less about the watchlist itself, but how we react to its implications; a world where we can't be our best, or most honest, selves.

Rebellion is tempting, but conformity is safer.

Watchlist was completed in mid-2019 when I handed it to the director with a disclaimer that 'the ending is a little crazy'. I've spent the past few months watching as my darkest daydreams became news headlines—first the devastation of the Australian fires and then the explosion of a zoonotic virus. I've also watched as negligent politicians, and some truly mad social commentators, pointed the finger at 'greenies' and 'vegetarians'. I'm not sure how that works. Maybe the right is just ... wrong?

I've chosen not to soften the play, or rewrite it. The Roger in me advised caution, but Delia's rebellion stands.

I sometimes wonder if ... the next time

I'm called a tree-hugger, or a hippie, or a bleeding heart ... the next day I'm harassed for walking alone ... I'll find it in myself to be polite and indulgent. Or if I'll lash out.

And then, I wonder, what is really the sane response? And will I play nice if I know I'm being watched?

Alex Vickery-Howe

DIRECTOR'S NOTE

Boy meets girl. Girl awakens boy. Boy tries to change the world.

Basil has lost his father. His mother now wants him out of the house, leaving him unsure of where to go or what to do. A caterer at his father's funeral purposefully catches his eye. This is the catalyst for his 'enlightenment'.

As Basil discovers through his mysterious love interest Delia and his best friend Roger, we face a harsh environmental and political landscape. Tribes have formed and a demonstration, indeed a performance, of your political action is demanded of you. Roger performs the role of an informed leftie. One who is not only aware of important socio-political issues but who can also hold his own in any moscato-fuelled garden party discussion. He shares reputable content on social media and makes a conscious effort to recycle carefully and effectively. Delia,

on the other hand, is interested in action over performance and doesn't seek the same kind of recognition. For her, it is far more difficult to adopt the mask of one who is vulnerable and open to interpersonal connection.

Keen to avoid the Manic Pixie Dream Girl trope—one that gifts male characters in need of growth with a disposable, often damaged, woman to encounter then leave behind as a quirky chapter in their memoirs—Vickery-Howe has created a complex love story between Basil and Delia. Theirs is a relationship marred by secrecy and distrust, with each of their respective premeditated intentions called into question. However, their connection is enough to permanently change Basil and at least challenge the steadfast Delia into thinking about it. As she admits towards the end of the play, 'I wasn't supposed to like you this much.'

Despite the challenge presented by her feelings for Basil, Delia remains resolute. The stakes are too high for her to back away now. The play calls into question personal and collective responsibility. To whom, or what, do we owe our attention, care and protection? For Delia, it's every living thing. A sentiment shared between her and Basil's father, Howard, who believed lizards to be as cute as kittens. But if you care for every living thing, take on every living thing's pain and suffering, how can you function? As Basil laments: (tapping his head) 'I see the world through her eyes now. I see pigs on spits, and remember that pigs are smarter than dogs. I see fur coats and imagine the horror of being born to be skinned ... You can't live in this world with all of those screams echoing in here.' Like Basil, we are overwhelmed. His eyes are opened to passion and courage but also to horror and cruelty. Delia's practical, radical activism, coupled with Roger's well-meaning but ultimately ineffective philosophising complements Basil's bewildering 'awakening'.

The desire to care, indeed to act, is often trumped by the paralysis of fear, uncertainty or convenience. We perform mental gymnastics to remove ourselves from exploitation, conflict and destruction. It's easier to say I don't know how to make a difference because there's so much that needs changing ... 'I'm only one person.' Despite Australia's ranking as one of the highest per capita emitters of carbon, the country's weak climate change policy, if you can even call it that, often relies on the argument that reductions won't make enough of a global impact while other large nations continue pumping carbon into the air. 'What's the point?' It's easier to forget that foie gras is the result of a disturbing and cruel process of torture or that beef is in fact dead cow, or that racehorses are sent to the knackery for slaughter ...

Watchlist is a fun and fierce contemporary call-to-arms which engages with the big and small picture. It challenges its characters and audiences to look beyond their own lives and engage with the high-stakes global issues of carbon emissions, environmental devastation and the destruction of our planet, its species and resources. It's a lot to take in but as Roger, in one of his more sincere moments declares, 'If you want to be real, you must start by opening those sleepy eyes of yours. Take a look at the wider world.'

Lisa Harper Campbell

A NOTE ON CONTEXT

It was science fiction movies that first exposed us to the vision of moving crowds where each person was trailed meekly by a text box with their name and other critical personal data. Now, that type of footage features on documentaries about China and how facial-recognition and phone tracking has Big Brother able to follow our every move.

Back home, we've come a long way since ASIO files on activists consisted of manila folders with blurry black and white photos taken surreptitiously from behind the potted palm. Now, you can't show your face in public without it being captured by hundreds of cameras capable of identifying you.

Those of us who have ever rocked the boat, and challenged the status quo for a cause, suspect that we're probably on a watchlist or ten. Is that why we pull our punches and (mostly) behave well? Or is it that we don't care quite enough? Or is Roger right? 'When we see something wrong, we turn away, we keep driving, we wait for some ... mythical grown-up to take care of it. We're weak.'

As activists from Extinction Rebellion ramp up their civil disobedience campaign and make us late for meetings by blocking roads, we are torn between admiration and anger. Are they the grown-ups we've been waiting for or just a bloody nuisance?

'Why couldn't you have joined the RSPCA like a normal person?'

Watchlist also skirts around nature and nurture. As Basil finds out more about his roots, perhaps he's a case of the apple not falling far from the tree? Or perhaps his interest in skirt is more hormonal? After all, the Children of God cult in the '70s and '80s successfully used Flirty Fishing to swell their ranks. Why not other causes?

Whether it's the things we do for love, an undiscovered 'activist gene' or a completely rational response to a terminally ill planet that leads us to the final shocking scene, is for us to decide. With more and more people realising that politeness and complacency won't move mountains and sitting on the fence won't save the world, maybe we should buckle in for a more turbulent ride ahead?

Mark Parnell MLC
Greens Member of the South Australian Parliament

ALEX VICKERY-HOWE
PLAYWRIGHT

Alex Vickery-Howe is an award-winning playwright and screenwriter. In 2008 he made his writing debut with *Once Upon a Midnight*, a bilingual, bicultural horror rock musical in Okinawa, Japan, where it opened the Kijimuna Festival (now Ricca Ricca Festival) and played to rave reviews and full houses, before selling out again at the Adelaide OzAsia Festival. He has subsequently written for a number of Australian theatre companies. On screen, Alex has written and directed short films which have played to a variety of international festivals. He holds a PhD from Flinders University, where he specialises in writing internationally for younger audiences.

LISA HARPER CAMPELL
DIRECTOR

Lisa Harper Campbell is an acting graduate of the Flinders University Drama Centre. Acting highlights include performing in the award-nominated *Biography: A Game* and *Perplex* (Joh Hartog Productions), appearing in new web-series *Ruby June*, and playing Julie Bishop in the national tour of *Abbott! The Musical*. She has also performed and toured her own original work including a comedic solo show, *A Bee's Dick Away*, and the satirical piece *A Full English Breakfast* with Clive Palmer. Lisa has produced for both theatre (Foul Play Theatre's *Julie and Yerma*) and radio (Radio Adelaide's Arts Breakfast). She has worked with acclaimed French actor and director Zabou Breitman and in 2019, made her directorial debut with *The Double Bass*. TV credits include winning Fastest Finger First on *Millionaire Hot Seat* and taking home the big brass mug on ABC's *Hard Quiz* with her special topic, the French Resistance. Lisa obtained her doctorate in French Cinema in 2017 and has since conducted research and lectured across French, Screen and Drama Studies at various universities. In the future, Lisa hopes to create and deliver many wildly appreciated, big budget plays, TV shows and films which explore socio-political issues with a comedic bent.

LUCY COMBE
PRODUCER

Lucy Combe is a writer, teacher and the Creative Producer of South Australian Playwrights Theatre. She graduated from Adelaide University in 1999 and subsequently founded Newfangled Productions as well as working on the Performing Arts Market and WOMADelaide for Arts Projects Australia. For many years she lived in the UK and worked in a range of positions for arts organisations, including administration, communication, recruitment, client services and marketing. She has a Grad. Dip. in Creative Writing from Birkbeck, University of London. In Melbourne, she worked with Western Edge Youth Arts (WEYA), assisting young refugees in the writing of *Old Ghosts, New Land* for the Big West Festival. For SA Playwrights Theatre, Lucy wrote and produced *The Middle Way* and produced Matt Hawkins' *Bordertown* in 2019.

STEPHEN DEAN
LIGHTING DESIGNER

Stephen Dean has been designing theatrical lighting for many decades and runs his own technical services production company, BallyHoo Productions, in addition to being Senior Venue Technician/Designer for the Bakehouse Theatre in Adelaide. Recent lighting designs include STARC's *A Night At The Theatre*, SA Playwrights' *Bordertown* and *The Double Bass* by Cranking Hog Productions. He has worked for Hunter Valley Summer Theatre and designed for productions of *Macbeth*, *How I Met My Mother* and *Devil's Caress* at the Factory Space Theatre in Sydney. Known for exploring innovative new lighting solutions, Stephen has worked across London and Edinburgh. He also writes for *CX Magazine* and his own blog, *Ramblings of a Techie*.

SASCHA BUDIMSKI
SOUND DESIGNER

Sascha Budimski is an Adelaide-based sound artist whose style of music involves mashing electronic beats, glitched acoustic instruments and textured ambiences. He developed his interest in sound art and electronic music while studying dance at the Adelaide College of the Arts, and he is drawn to designing and creating sound for theatre, dance and art installations. Sascha is a qualified sound engineer with a Diploma of Music Industry from the School of Audio Engineering (SAE) in Adelaide, where he developed a love for recording and mixing bands and musicians. Works featuring his sound design have received awards and nominations, including several Australian Dance Awards, South Australian Small Screen Awards and a nomination in the 2018 Performing Arts WA Awards for his composition for *Love/Less* by Kynan Hughes. Recently, Sascha's work has received international attention in shows presented in Germany, Spain, Belgium, Denmark and Sweden. To hear examples of his work visit www.svb-audio.com

CLARE MIYUKI GUERIN
STAGE MANAGER

Clare Miyuki Guerin is an Adelaide-based stage manager, graduating from Adelaide College of the Arts in 2018 with an Advanced Diploma of Live Production and Management Services. Since graduating, Clare has served as an ASM for *End of the Rainbow* and *A View From The Bridge*, both with STCSA. She has worked for the Adelaide Festival Centre Trust as part of the OzAsia Festival, for State Opera South Australia on *Hamlet*, and as stage manager and technical operator for independent theatre production *Limit* at The Bakehouse Theatre. Clare has also found success internationally, stage managing a number of musicals, plays, and performance art pieces. While in Tokyo, Clare also worked as a voice actor, audition coach, dancing beer can, and Japanese to English translator and interpreter. She is thrilled to be part of the *Watchlist* production team.

GIANLUCA NOBLE
BASIL

Gianluca Noble graduated from Flinders University Drama Centre with First Class Honours and a University Medal in 2019. Previous credits include *Flood* and *Blink* (The Cabbages and Kings Collective); *Julius Caesar*, *Moth*, *Shoot/Get Treasure/Repeat*, *Other Times*, *Three Sisters*, and *Our Town* (Flinders University Drama Centre). In July 2020 he will attend the Arthaus Berlin International Summer School in devised theatre with the support of a Carclew Fellowship. He has also worked offstage as a producer and production manager in multiple productions at the Adelaide Fringe Festival.

KATIE O'REILLY
MARIE

Since graduating from Flinders Drama Centre in 2000, Katie O'Reilly has worked successfully interstate, overseas and locally, on screen and stage. Some TV highlights have been playing Amelia Moon on *Neighbours* (Channel 10), guest roles on *Stingers* (Channel 9) and *Blue Heelers* (Channel 7). While living in Ireland she had an ongoing role on RTE's long running soap *Fair City* playing Zora McCarthy. Film credits include *Caterpillar Wish* and *Fatty Finn*. Katie is a member of South Australian Playwrights Theatre. Recent theatre credits include their production of *Bordertown* and *The Middle Way*, both performed at Holden Street Theatre. Katie also has a working relationship with Irish Theatre Company, Sunday's Child and performed with them in *Nuclear Family* at the 2017 Adelaide Fringe.

KATHERINE SORTINI
DELIA

Katherine Sortini is a 2018 Honours graduate from the Flinders Drama Centre. She is an actor, dancer and theatre-maker who founded the independent theatre company Deus Ex Femina. Her theatre credits include *Our Town*, *The Three Sisters*, *Other Times*, *Shoot/Get Treasure/Repeat*, *Moth* and *Julius Caesar* (Flinders University Drama Centre), *Flood* (The Cabbages and Kings Collective), *The Promise* (Holden Street Theatres), *The Wolves* (RUMPUS), *Bordertown* (South Australian Playwrights Theatre) and *Gaslight* (State Theatre Company of South Australia). Her film credits include Daria in *Truth Will Out* and Azura in *Ruby June*. Her TV credits include *Upright* and *Haley*. Katherine is a proud member of Actors Equity.

EDDIE MORRISON
ROGER

Eddie Morrison graduated from AC Arts in 2008. Since then, he has worked extensively in theatre and film, including a national tour of *Mr. McGee And The Biting Flea* with Patch, writing and performing with comedy troupe The Golden Phung, and featuring as Hermann Goering in *Danger 5* for SBS. He premiered his self-devised solo show, *The Best Show*, in the 2019 Adelaide Fringe. Most recently, Eddie appeared acting and playing double bass in the State Theatre Company of South Australia's production of *End Of The Rainbow* by Peter Quilter and under the banner of Cranking Hog Productions, he gave a critically acclaimed performance in Patrick Süskind's solo show *The Double Bass*. Eddie is a proud member of Actor's Equity.

MATT HAWKINS
NORMAN

Matt Hawkins is a playwright, screenwriter, lecturer and actor. He has spent the last 20 years not only writing and directing his own projects but also developing the work of young actors and screenwriters. He has written extensively for the stage and television in Australia, UK and Ghana. His credits include *Always Greener* (7 Network), *Life Support* (SBS) and *The Micallef Program* (ABC). He was script editor, writer and show runner for the hit Ghanaian TV series *Different Shades of Blue* (GTV - Sparrow Productions). He wrote the critically acclaimed plays *Bordertown* and *Frank Forbes and the Yahoo Boy*.

www.ingramcontent.com/pod-product-compliance
Lightning Source LLC
Chambersburg PA
CBHW050016090426
42734CB00021B/3289